THE SECRET FORMULA TO STOP BABY FEEDING AVERSION

UNLOCK THE HIDDEN METHOD TO SATISFYING YOUR BABY'S HUNGER TO CEASE PPD ASSOCIATED WITH BREASTFEEDING AVERSION, BOTTLED FEEDING AVERSION, AND CLUSTER FEEDING

KIMBERLY NICOLE WHITTAKER

D1203061

INTRODUCTION

You just became a mother!

It's the most joyous occasion for every parent, **especially** for a mother who has gone through a life and death experience while giving birth to her baby.

You may now be thinking *that the difficult time is over, and now I just need to feed my baby, and he'll grow himself.*

But, *No!* Sorry – that's not the case.

Have you thought about feeding a baby?

It looks so simple. All you have to do is put your breast in his tender little mouth, and when he's grown a bit, you'll just need to make food for him, and he'll eat and grow and *voila*! Everything will be done. My dear, let me tell you that feeding a baby is not like that!

Feeding a baby can seem like the **most challenging thing** on earth for a mom.

From the very first moment after becoming a mother, many things may rush through your mind:

- How will I feed my baby?
- Will my breasts provide enough milk to suffice his hunger?
- How do I hold my baby for feeding?
- Should I start with bottle feeding?
- What are the best times to feed my baby?
- What if I forget to feed him on time?
- What if my baby doesn't accept my breastmilk?
- How do I choose the right formula?
- When should I go for formula feeding?
- When should I start giving solids to my baby?
- How do I introduce table foods to my baby?
- How do I choose the right foods for my baby?
- Should I go for paced feeding?

And the list goes on and on...

Now, this is looking so scary to you. Isn't it? But don't worry. What if I told you that I had experienced almost all the problems listed above myself? I'm a mother of three young ones, and there are tons of solutions for each of these issues. Through my experience and extensive research, I have written this book so that all moms can be super right from the start.

I was about to give up breastfeeding because it was so **tiresome and exhausting**. I didn't know what to do and where to go when my baby suddenly started crying in the middle of the night just after I'd fed her for 30 minutes with body pain and swollen eyes dying to sleep. But I kept going and never gave up.

Luckily! I believed that *"Every problem comes with many solutions"* and remained determined. I worked hard to find those solutions, and I found them. These ideas and solutions were life-changing as they made my life so much easier. I persevered with getting rid of each problem as the days progressed, and I thought of myself as if I were a **PRO MOM**.

What if I help you become so good at feeding your baby that you will not even think of giving up as I did? That's what this book is all about. I don't want you to face the problems I had while breastfeeding and feeding my children solids. Now you look **relieved**. You should be! In this book, I'll tell you all about breastfeeding along with other nutritional feedings you can introduce when the baby is big enough. I'll give you advice for babies up to two years old. I'll also discuss the best formulas for bottle feeding and the best foods for your baby when he/she can start eating solids. Plus, I'll teach you how to make delicious, nutritious baby foods at home.

I will address all the stages of feeding a baby, problems related to every stage, and their solutions, along with some life-saving hacks which will prevent you from falling into anxiety and many other health issues. Here's what you will discover:

- **Preparing** yourself for breastfeeding even before giving birth
- **Problems** with breastfeeding and their proven solutions
- **What to do if the baby doesn't accept** your milk
- **Which solid foods to use** and when you can start giving them to your baby
- **How to avoid** falling into anxiety, depression, and other health issues
- **How to handle criticism** of not being able to feed your baby
- **How to prevent exhaustion** from endless nursing
- **How to handle a baby** who refuses to take food
- **What nutrients** are required for your baby, and at what age?
- **How to choose the correct formula** for bottle feeding your baby
- What a **breastmilk bank** is and how to find one
- How to make **baby food**
- What are **nipple confusion** and **nipple inversion?**
- **How to keep a check** on whether your baby is getting an adequate diet
- **What behavioral signs** you should keep an eye on while feeding him
- **All the essential foods you need** to feed your baby with a proper age division chart
- **What not to feed** your baby at all
- **Medical recommendations** about the health and diet of mother and baby
- **Time management** information about feeding your baby so he won't go hungry for too long
- **What feeding disorders are** and how they can be prevented

As a mother, I have documented all the problems I faced while feeding my baby till she became two years old. These are just brief outlines of what you'll find in this book, and then some. I have tried to write about every aspect of feeding during the long, tiring, and sometimes scary first two years.

You may be wondering why I'm so confident about it...

There's just **one reason** – I have been through all this, and there is no one better to write about an issue than one who has experienced everything about it.

I have helped some of my friends and family who have recently become mothers themselves. You know what? They often call me **SUPER MOM** because I've saved them from so many difficulties and endless pain.

It is my promise to every mother out there that reading this book and applying what it says will make your life heavenly peaceful, and you'll get rid of your feeding problems from the start of the first page.

Oh no!

I just reminded you of all the problems you may encounter while feeding your baby which may include exhaustion, pain, sleeplessness, personal life matters, disturbing chores, confusion about the selection of food, not knowing how to make baby food, and much more, when I was trying to be motivational and solve all your problems!

But this reminder was on purpose because that's what will happen if you keep waiting and telling yourself that you don't need this.

BREASTFEEDING

*E*very mother is familiar with what breastfeeding is, but many are unaware of its necessity and importance. Most just think of it as a straightforward procedure and ignore the problems and difficulties it may cause for both mother and baby.

Breastfeeding can be the most delightful experience for the mother because if it goes well, it gives her all the confidence that she needs to become a good mom and stay healthy both mentally and physically.

Your breasts are the milk-producing organ that consists of two parts. One is outside the body, round and large. The second is inside the body and is made up of various ducts and mammary glands. The outer part has a small outgrowth called the nipple that the milk comes out of. The nipple is surrounded by darker pigmented skin that is called the areola.

Milk production is stimulated when your baby starts sucking on the areola. Your brain gets the message that the baby is hungry, and by the power of specific hormones, the mammary glands begin to produce milk. In the very first week of nursing (aka breastfeeding), you may experience a tingling sensation in your breasts when the baby starts sucking on the nipples and areola. You may feel thirstier than usual so keep yourself well hydrated.

The milk you'll produce in the first 2 or 3 days will be rich in nutrients, proteins, and even antibodies. It is a yellowish color and comes out in small amounts because your baby's stomach is very tiny at first. He only needs a small amount of it. This first milk is called colostrum, and it needs to be fed to the baby 8 to 12 times in 24 hours.

Don't worry about the amount of milk you are producing in the first 2-3 days. It is usually very small in amount. On around the third or fourth day, you will start producing larger amounts of milk. People sometimes refer to this as your milk "coming in." It can take more time than this because it depends upon the hormones in your body. In some mothers, they act faster than others. Just keep letting your baby suckle every couple of hours as this will stimulate the milk production hormones.

So, usually, after 48 to 72 hours of becoming a mom, you'll start producing 'mature milk,' which is just like normal milk in color and texture.

Every drop of your milk is perfectly composed of all the nutrients your baby needs. There is no such thing as breastmilk being "too weak" as some people believe.

BENEFITS OF BREASTMILK FOR BABY

According to science, breastmilk is the best food source for a baby for the first six months as it contains all the essential nutrients in properly balanced amounts. It has all the components necessary to improve the baby's immune system and offer protection for the baby's internal body system. It also contains bioactive molecules that help the baby digest his food. Breastmilk imparts long-term benefits to the baby's health and allows him to develop a mature immune system for fighting against infections such as viruses.

It is recommended that a baby should be fed only breastmilk in his first six months. No other foods or liquids (juices and formula) should be given to the baby. But this only happens in an ideal situation but is not very common. It's unique with every mother and child, and it's solely your decision if you want to breastfeed your baby or not. However, if you decide to formula feed your baby, remember that he does not need any solid food for the first six months or so. Introducing solids too early can lead to problems like obesity and allergies.

breastmilk contains all the essential nutrients that your baby's body needs and helps his bones and organs grow. These minerals include calcium, sodium, potassium, magnesium, beneficial fats, and protein.

If I start listing the benefits of breastfeeding, it would require me to write another book, so I'll just share the most important ones here.

One significant benefit is that it contains a proper mixture of vitamins, proteins, and fats, all the things needed for a baby's growth. It's also the best way to develop closeness and love between yourself and your baby as it contains body-to-body touch, eye contact, and physical nearness.

breastmilk protects your baby from illness and reduces the risk of many medical issues such as:

• Diabetes

• Obesity

• Certain cancers

• Infections

• Incorrect bone development

• Diarrhea

• Allergies

• Becoming underweight

BENEFITS OF BREASTFEEDING FOR THE MOTHER

No doubt breastfeeding is the most important thing for a newborn baby, but it also has many positive effects on the mother both physically and emotionally. It is good for the mother's health, and it prevents her from falling into any emotional trauma due to not being able to feed her little one.

Breastfeeding is not just a procedure of giving food to your baby; it's far more than that. It provides the best bonding connection between mother and baby. Mothers who breastfeed their babies seem to be healthier, happier, and more relaxed than those who don't. They develop a special connection with their babies.

Don't worry if you cannot breastfeed – it doesn't mean your baby won't get close to you. It's just one of the benefits of breastfeeding; the closeness of baby and mother also depends upon hundreds of other factors as well.

Breastfeeding will help you burn calories which is very healthy as it helps you lose the weight you gained during pregnancy. It releases the hormone oxytocin, which prevents excessive uterine bleeding after birth and quickly helps your uterus get back in shape. Breastfeeding also lowers the chances of breast cancer and osteoporosis.

One more important benefit is that you won't have the expense of buying milk bottles, milk formulas, or the stress of making them. You also won't have to worry about sterilizing nipples and bottles. It will save you both money and time and will keep you stress-free, allowing you to spend quality time with your cute baby.

SIGNS THAT SHOW YOUR BABY IS HUNGRY

The most problematic thing for new moms is that they wonder how they will know if their baby is hungry and when to feed them. They also worry that they might not know about the baby's appetite, and he may go unfed for a long time.

Don't worry! There are some signs which will tell you that your baby needs to be fed:

• Sticking out tongue

• Licking their fingers

• Moving their heads

• Nudging against your breast

• Rooting reflex – they try to take everything in their mouth which touches their cheeks.

• Opening their mouths again and again

• Tries to put everything in their mouth

• Licking their lips

• Crying

You have to keep a check on these signs, so your baby gets milk on time and remains healthy.

Newborn babies should be fed 8-12 times in the first few weeks. Occasionally babies go on napping for a long time without feeding, but you have to wake them up and feed them so they won't go hungry. This will help them to get the nutrients their bodies need to grow. In the first few weeks, you even have to wake them up at night and feed them every 3-4 hours if they don't wake themselves. Once they're a little older, they should sleep all night long because sleeping helps the baby grow.

Similarly, there are things you should keep an eye on to know whether your baby is getting sufficient milk or not.

• Should not lose more than 7 % of their birth weight in the first few weeks.

• He will stay calm after 3-4 hours of feeding because his stomach will be full.

• Should pee at regular intervals, around 5-6 times a day, with clear or pale-colored pee.

BREASTFEEDING POSITIONS

The best breastfeeding position is the one you and your baby find most comfortable and relaxing. So, this is up to you to find that one. This position will be one which you'll not find tiring, and you'll not become overwhelmed by holding the baby for too long.

You can observe how other moms handle their babies while feeding and then practice it by yourself. You will get exhausted from breastfeeding and develop a sore back if you don't find a comfortable position. Sometimes you have to change the position of breastfeeding depending upon the situation you are in.

You may be tired from working and not have the energy to sit and hold the baby in the cradle position. You can then use the lying-down position.

The following are the most commonly used breastfeeding positions:

- Cradle position

This is the most common breastfeeding position, and you'll probably use this position from the very first day. Every mother is familiar with this way of sitting.

Make your arm into a crook shape and rest the side of the baby's head on it with his body facing your face. Fully attach the baby's belly to your lower chest so he'll feel more supported. You can wrap around your other arm, so the baby's head and back get more support.

Now cup your other hand around the breast, squeeze the areola gently, and put it into the baby's mouth. Make sure the entire nipple and part of the areola are in his mouth. He should start sucking to get his food. If you only put the nipple into the baby's mouth, your nipple will become very sore.

- Football hold position

This position is best suited for newborns in their first few weeks because they cannot hold their heads steady themselves. It is also best suited for mothers who have had a cesarean birth while their wound is still fresh. It will prevent you from putting the baby's weight on your belly so that it will hurt less.

This position requires holding the baby like a football, supporting his head and neck, and aligning him with your arm, i.e., the baby's back should go along your forearm. This will support his back, and you can hold his head steady with your hand.

- Side-lying position

You are tired and exhausted from a long day of nursing and working, and you just need to lie down and sleep. Now you suddenly remember you have to feed your baby. At times like this, it's difficult to get up and sit in a chair to feed your baby.

Don't worry – I'll tell you about a side-lying position which you can use while lying down.

This position is excellent for mothers recovering from an episiotomy (a cut made to widen the vagina for birth) because lying down is less painful than sitting on the stitches.

Put a pillow under your head so you can relax. Next, lean your baby towards your breast, squeeze the areola, and put it and the nipple in the baby's mouth. Make sure the baby is correctly latched on, and then support his head and neck with your free hand so the nipple won't twist. You can support the baby and your arm with another pillow if this is comfortable. Remember to always lift the baby towards your breast rather than leaning down towards him. Keep on nursing until your baby is full.

- Laid-back position

This position is also called biological nurturing because it's just as nature has made the breastfeeding process for both mother and child. It seems to be a naturally driven position. It is more relaxing for you and your baby as you'll both be lying down in a suitable, relaxed position.

Lean back with a pillow or two against your back, or just use the bed's headboard. You should have proper support for your head and back to avoid back or neck pain. Hold your baby and lie him down so that his tummy is facing your tummy. Let your baby choose the most accessible position for him as long as his cheeks are resting near your breast. Help your baby put the nipple in his mouth and have a good latch-on to feed properly.

- Cross-cradle position

This position is slightly different from the simple cradle position. Some moms find this more relaxing and suitable for breastfeeding.

You will sit straight and get comfortable. You can use a chair with armrests. Hold your baby in the crook of your arm opposite the breast you will use for feeding. Support his head and neck. Bring your baby towards your body so that his belly is against yours.

With your other hand, cup your breast in a U-shaped grip. Put the nipple and areola into the baby's mouth and bring him closer so that he can latch on.

Remember not to lean forward in this position but bring the baby up towards you.

SOME BASIC TIPS FOR BREASTFEEDING

There are some proven and tips you need to know before starting breastfeeding. These will help you in your breast-feeding experience.

- Skin-to-skin touch

This is the most important thing to remember when starting breastfeeding. Skin-to-skin touch will improve the bond between child and mother. It will give you a sense of closeness and affection towards the baby. He will feel more comfortable, and it will create a desirable atmosphere for breastfeeding. This will be so soothing for you and your baby. It will improve your breastfeeding experience, and your baby will feed more.

- Your smell matters

Your body smell matters a lot while breastfeeding. Your newborn should get the good smell of your milk in starting few days so he can get used to it. You should use simple soaps and not put on scented perfumes or other strong fragrances that make it difficult for the baby to smell your milk and breast.

You might want to limit the number of people who hold your baby in the first 2 or 3 weeks until the mature milk starts coming and breastfeeding has been well established.

- Make eye contact

Some mothers start watching TV or scrolling on their mobile phones while feeding their babies. You should not do that, especially in the first few weeks of motherhood. This might not seem important, but believe me, it is a big deal as it has excellent benefits in the long run.

Instead, use the time to stare deeply into your baby's eyes. It will develop a deeper connection between the two of you. Science recommends that staring at your baby while breastfeeding increases your hormonal activity and your milk production increases.

- Rest is important

Many mothers ignore the fact that they should be well-rested before breastfeeding. If you are exhausted, breastfeeding will become difficult for you and may not produce enough milk. You should stay in bed more than normal as it will make breastfeeding much more manageable. Try to take a power nap while your baby is napping during the day.

If possible, get some help with your household chores and do not rush into doing everything. Household duties are less important than taking care of your baby. Not getting proper rest while you are a breastfeeding mother can lead to many problems. For example, breast infections like mastitis, postpartum depression, and fatigue.

- Be patient

Your newborns are just little souls who just came to this enormous world. Like you, they will take time to learn how to breastfeed, and they may take a longer time to breastfeed. Usually, a baby takes 10 to 30 minutes to get enough milk.

Some babies may take longer than this time. If they are slow, you will need to be patient and in control. Don't rush your baby to stop feeding after a few minutes; let him decide when he is full.

- Proper latch-on

A proper latch is as essential for breastfeeding as the milk itself. The baby should be properly latched to get the most milk and doesn't hurt you. Both baby lips should be squeezed outward around your nipple and should touch the dark area around the nipple called the areola.

Your baby should do a **deep latch**. You would be wondering what on earth that is. It is very simple. Hold your breast with your thumb and index finger near the edges of the areola, forming a C shape or U-shaped cup with your hand. Bring the thumb and finger closer by gently squeezing your breast. Keep your fingers at the sides, making a formation like a half sandwich.

Now hold the baby's head firmly with your other hand supporting his head and neck. Bring the baby close to the nipple, resting it near the baby's upper lip. The baby should open his mouth wide to suck. Gently push the baby's head towards the breast to place his upper jaw well behind the nipple. Keep pushing your breast with the thumb.

Wait for a few seconds, and once a deep latch has been established, the baby will start sucking.

The infant should have the complete nipple in his mouth so that he can properly suck. Latching on should be perfectly done because it will protect you from pain and sore nipples.

NO BREASTFEEDING IN THESE CIRCUMSTANCES

There are some medical and physical conditions in which breastfeeding is prohibited because it can harm your child. First of all, you should consult your pediatrician before starting breastfeeding because he's the one who has all of your reports to clear you for breastfeeding.

Following are the cases in which breastfeeding is strictly prohibited unless a doctor has cleared you:

1. If you have HIV, it can be transferred to your baby through breastmilk

2. You have cancer and are getting chemotherapy for it

3. You have been suffering from prolonged TB (tuberculosis)

4. You are addicted to drugs like cocaine or marijuana

5. Your baby has galactosemia, a condition in which his body is unable to digest and tolerate the natural sugars present in breastmilk

6. You're on medical drugs, needed for any kind of illness

Having flu or cough-like conditions should not prevent you from feeding. It will have no harm on your baby, but it may transfer antibodies against them to your baby through milk which will help his immune system to become stronger.

Some infants do not feed properly, and they start becoming weaker day by day. In this case, you should consult a doctor and ask him to prescribe supplements for your baby, especially iron and vitamin K. These are the most important supplements to be given to infants if they are not breastfeeding properly.

COMMON BREASTFEEDING CHALLENGES AND THEIR SOLUTIONS

While most mothers find breastfeeding a breeze once they've got the hang of it, it can be a nightmare for some mothers. They may have to face some challenges, which can lead to some physical as well as medical issues. Let us discuss them one by one, and I'll help you with some solutions.

1. Cracked and sore nipples

When you start breastfeeding, cracked and sore nipples may develop.

Causes:

• The baby is not properly latched on while feeding

• No proper relaxing technique or position for breastfeeding

• Using breast pumps

• Chafing against clothes due to wet nipples after feeding

• Tissue damage or skin cut

OCCASIONALLY CRACKED or sore nipples occur in the first few weeks of breastfeeding. This happens to almost every mother at one time or another, but don't worry because there are tons of solutions.

Treatment:

• Apply a corticosteroid lotion right after you finish breastfeeding the baby, but only for a few days. Using steroids for too long can cause thinning of the skin around the nipples. Consult a medical professional before using them. Wash it off before a feed so that the baby will not ingest any.

- Apply emollient creams that contain lanolin or coconut oil to your nipples. This will help the skin to soften and will help to heal soreness and cracks.
- Some mothers even apply their breastmilk to the cracked nipples. Let it dry before putting your clothes back on. It can protect against cracking as it has many antibacterial properties.
- For avoiding friction on nipples, do not wear bras that are too tight.
- Do not use deodorants, powders, harsh soaps, and other things like this, which can dry and crack the skin around your nipples and cause them to be sensitive. Instead, use plain warm water to wash your breasts after every feeding session.
- Feed exclusively with one breast for the whole feed to give the other nipple a break and time to heal. At the next feed, switch to the other breast.

DO NOT STOP BREASTFEEDING if you get sore or cracked nipples. Remember that breastfeeding is the most important thing for your baby, and he must get it. Some pain is normal while breast-feeding, and you'll have to work through it. It will go away with time once you continue feeding.

1. Inverted nipples

Some women have inverted nipples, and others develop them later. This means that instead of sticking out, they point inward or lie flat. It can happen in one breast or both. Maybe you are born with it or may have developed it when you started breast-feeding as a medical condition.

Inverted nipples can be simple to severe. You may experience simple or grade 1 nipple inversion in which the nipple can be pulled outward easily, or they stay outward for some time on their own. You can breastfeed easily in this condition.

You may also experience grade 2 nipple inversion in which the nipples can be pulled outwards but go back inward quickly. Breastfeeding becomes difficult in this condition.

With a severe or grade 3 condition, the nipples cannot be pulled outwards. You may not be able to breastfeed in this condition.

Causes:

- Aging
- Breast injury or surgery
- Naturally inverted nipples from birth
- Mammary duct ectasia (ducts carrying milk can expand or become blocked) Mastitis (a bacterial infection of the breasts)

Treatment:

- Nipple inversion devices
- Surgery
- Hoffman technique – this works most of the time if you have grade 1 or 2 nipple inversion. You

simply have to put your thumbs at the sides of your nipples and start pulling them downwards by applying gentle pressure. Repeat it on all the sides of the nipples. This technique will help your nipples to stand out.

1. Breast engorgement

It is normal when your breasts become full of milk with flattened nipples but remain relatively soft and flexible. However, some women find that they become painfully full, especially in the first week after childbirth when milk production begins. It's caused by an increased blood supply to the breasts as well as the milk itself. The breasts become painfully swollen and overfull.

Treatment:

- Washing breasts with warm water or taking steam showers with gentle squeezing breasts can remove these clogs. Try putting hot face cloths on your breasts for 10 minutes at a time. (Not too hot...you don't want to burn yourself!)
- Squeezing your breasts to release milk and feeding the baby regularly can also help you get rid of breast engorgement. You can also use a breast pump for this. Be careful not to completely empty your breasts though or they will produce even more.
- Try feeding the baby smaller amounts more frequently, for instance, every 2 hours. Massage your breasts gently with a mild oil for lubrication.

If the condition becomes worse, you will have to consult a specialist for treatment.

1. Breast infection

Sometimes when sore or cracked nipples remain there for a long time, they may develop a breast infection known as mastitis. Bacteria enter through cracked nipples and cause this infection.

Symptoms:

A sore, red area around the nipples, flu-like symptoms, fever, fatigue, pain while breastfeeding.

Treatment:

You need to go to the doctor. Usually, antibiotics are prescribed to treat the infection. Apply moist heat to the sore area to get relief from breast soreness. You can continue breastfeeding with a mild breast infection.

1. Blocked ducts

The ducts that carry the milk in your breasts can also become clogged and blocked. You'll feel a sore lumpy spot on your breast. It can be red and hot.

Treatment:

This can be treated by gently massaging the sore area of the breast. More frequent breastfeeding can also help you get rid of blocked milk ducts. Rub the area as the baby sucks to try to clear the blockage.

1. Stress and anxiety

You can get tired and stressed out from continued nursing of your baby. This can lead to anxiety and other health issues. It is more difficult at the start to cope with the tiredness of breast-feeding because you have to work so hard to get it right.

Try to stay calm and relaxed because this tiresome journey is the most important thing for your baby's health. Sleep well and avoid working too hard and wasting your energy on household tasks. Accept offers of help with household tasks and shopping and just focus on nursing your baby, especially in the first few months of motherhood. This will give you more time to rest and stay focused to prevent you from falling into issues like stress, anxiety, or depression.

SELF-CARE WHILE BREASTFEEDING

They say, *'If you are healthy, your infant will be healthier'*. This is so true because an infant's health depends upon the health of the mother as he is feeding on the mother's milk. To achieve this, you must take care of yourself and maintain your health for continuing a healthy breastfeeding life. Self-care should be prioritized so that the baby's health is prioritized. You can take care of yourself in the following ways:

• Eat healthy meals 3 times a day.

• Keep your food portions in check and make sure you are getting all the nutrients. • Increase the number of dairy foods in your diet.

• You should have 3 servings of protein-rich food each day.

• Eat 3-4 servings of fruits each day.

• Eat at least 5 servings of vegetables a day.

• Drink more fluids. Water is best. Avoid sugary drinks and all alcohol.

• Start exercising regularly to keep yourself fit and active.

• Avoid drinking alcohol, too much caffeine, and smoking because they affect your milk.

BREASTFEEDING AVERSION

*B*reastfeeding Aversion and Agitation (BAA) is a special issue that some breastfeeding mamas have. It comprises having specific negative feelings, typically including invasive thoughts when the baby is latching and sucking on her breast.

These feelings are typically abrupt and nearly always undesirable, and numerous mamas who face this condition would like to pursue breastfeeding. If you have breastfeeding aversion, you will experience feelings of:

- Irritability
- Irritation
- Disgust
- Skin itching/ crawling
- Wrath
- Embarrassment and guilt (mostly afterward)

Intrusive thoughts are known to happen in motherhood. However, with nipple aversion, these seem to be specific to breastfeeding and might include:

- You want to run away so that they cannot breastfeed
- A devastating desire to stop breastfeeding
- You feel stuck or feel like that you are a prisoner
- You want to pinch your baby, so it will stop feeding
- Feelings and thoughts of being "touched out"

These sentiments vanish when the newborn baby stops breastfeeding, and he is not latching anymore.

You may feel a sense of guilt due to the intrusive thoughts and negative sentiments/feelings. Many mamas do not tell anybody how they're feeling and battle with an internal conflict of wanting to breastfeed but once they've committed to it, they undergo aversion towards it. A few mamas want to stop nursing altogether due to breastfeeding aversion if their condition is extreme and long-lasting, or if they don't know what it is. This too can cause sentiments of guilt about stopping breastfeeding before the mama and her newborn baby were prepared.

CAUSES OF BREASTFEEDING AVERSION AND AGITATION (BAA)

You may face this condition, but please don't feel you're alone. Most of the mamas who experience it don't know the reasons behind it. Breastfeeding Aversion and Agitation have definite causes, here are some of them:

- Hormones

A FEW MAMAS link the experience of breastfeeding aversion to their monthly cycle (menstruation) and experience it for many days every month. Once they have recognized this pattern and figured it out, it'll pass; it makes it easier to persevere. This determines that the cause may be hormonal for few ladies and may be comparative to pre-or post menstrual tension. Furthermore, it is probably hormonal for the mamas who get a period of breastfeeding aversion during their pregnancies as the body changes and the costs on a mother's body to fulfill both incubation and lactation possibly playing a part.

- Breastfeeding dynamic

Breastfeeding aversion can occur at any time but is more prevalent with older babies (aged between 12-24 months). As your baby grows older, his demand for milk and breastfeeding sessions increases even though he is doing well with solid foods. Sometimes babies demand breastfeeding for comfort even when they are not hungry.

THIS CAN LEAD to breastfeeding aversion in mamas. Here are some tips to avoid this; distract your baby with his favorite toy or something else that he enjoys more. You can take your baby to some fun places and even walking in the park sometimes helps. If your baby has settled with solid foods, consider weaning him off from breastfeeding.

- Self-care and sleep deprivation

The need for rest can influence us in many ways. Lack of sleep can cause chronic diseases including depression. You sometimes need to stay up all night to breastfeed and care for a small baby. Some mamas express their feelings about this and they say that it is difficult for them to breastfeed without resting properly. It is upsetting for them to maintain breastfeeding on demand at night because nighttime is for rest. When they do not get enough rest, it makes feeding difficult for them. Typically, many mamas are hit with a breastfeeding aversion when they do not get an adequate, nutritious diet and are not hydrating themselves sufficiently.

- Triggers

Not getting enough sleep or not having much time for self-care are the most common reasons given as triggers for a breastfeeding aversion. You may face the milder precursor of encounter aversion. This is the feeling of being 'touched out'. It refers to mamas who feel overwhelmed by all the physical contact with their newborn babies and having no time left for themselves without being touched.

THINGS A MOTHER DOESN'T EXPECT ABOUT BREASTFEEDING AVERSION

Many mamas are unaware of this syndrome and never expect that such a thing could happen to them. During BAA many negative feelings and challenges are faced by mothers.

- Aversion can strike at any point in any breastfeeding mom's journey

It is well known that aversion can strike both when a mama is pregnant, breastfeeding a newborn, or nursing an older child. It really can happen at any point along the breastfeeding journey. Few mamas encounter it at the newborn stage. There's a solid defense that aversion is a natural and biological trigger to start weaning older children. If the nursling is under 12 months and a mama encounters aversion then she needs to remember that her milk is the fundamental source of her baby's nutrition, so she needs to get some advice from a child specialist to help her continue.

- Mothers experiencing aversion do not always want to stop breastfeeding

When a breastfeeding mother is going through aversion, negative feelings like anger, agitation, skin-crawling sensations, and an overwhelming desire to stop nursing are triggered. She also feels like a prisoner whenever she breastfeeds, has negative thoughts that make her want to stop breastfeeding, and wants to run away. such moms become emotionally disturbed and stressed because they are experiencing BAA and don't feed their babies as they should. However, most of them want the aversion to go away.

- Aversion can be decreased or even go away for some mamas

Aversion can be helped for moms who

- Figure out their triggers
- Make variations to their routines and lifestyle
- Improve their sleeping routines
- Improve their hygiene
- Improve their eating habits
- Utilize supplements like magnesium, which can make aversion less severe or vanish
- Aversion is different from D-MER (Dysphoric Milk Ejection Reflex)

DYSPHORIC MILK EJECTION Reflex is a medical condition and it is diagnosed in a breastfeeding mom when her milk letdown causes her to feel negative feelings like depression, hopelessness, and despondency. It remains for a couple of minutes. This is different from aversion which remains throughout the whole feed whether it lasts two minutes or two hours.

- To stop breastfeeding can be as hard as carrying on

To stop breastfeeding can be tough for moms with an aversion because of the shame and guilt they experience. If mothers with aversion decide to stop breastfeeding, it is amazingly tough for them to do because they know that if they stop breastfeeding they may regret later not fulfilling their baby's needs.

- Oxytocin can cause BAA

A few mamas may have a negative affiliation to breastfeeding due to being a survivor of past sexual mishandling, childhood injury, or a challenging and painful start to their breastfeeding journey. Oxytocin typically plays a part in stress regulation. It can cause stress and uneasiness because it actuates a portion of the brain that heightens the memory. This means that past negative experiences can be brought up when the baby is feeding.

COPING WITH NURSING AVERSION

If you are battling with breastfeeding aversion, you will stress a lot due to the situations you are going through. You may feel tension and anxiety and even want to wean but you feel that you can't because you want the best for your baby. Here are a few ways you can reduce the feelings of aversion or even help it to disappear completely.

- Take care of yourself

You should take care and look out for yourself. Of course, a new mom is busy taking care of her baby and has little time for herself. However, it's important to take time to drink plenty of water, eat healthy food with enough calories, and sleep as much as you can. Try getting into the habit of keeping a pretty water jug and glass next to the place where you feed your baby. Keep a selection of healthy snacks, no-preparation on hand that you can just grab when you're feeling puckish. Things like grapes, strawberries, nuts, wholewheat crackers, and cheese need little preparation.

- Give yourself a little grace

You should not feel guilty about having such negative thoughts and feelings. Cheer yourself up with the thought that these feelings are natural and you are the perfect mama for your children. You are doing the best you can. Join a happy online chat group where you can socialize without leaving your house. Share your feelings with someone you trust. Changing your everyday routine by going on a trip or picnic can also help.

- Find a temporary distraction

When you are feeding your baby and feel any kind of anger, it is suggested that you find a temporary distraction. For example, once your baby is latched on, scroll your social media channels, watch videos on YouTube or Netflix, or turn on the television to distract yourself from negative thoughts until your baby has finished his feed.

- Set boundaries

Once your baby is a little older, you will need to set a schedule for him. You should not allow an older baby to completely rely on your breastmilk if they are hungry. Redirect him/her to other food.

You can also distract your baby by engaging them in different activities like playing games if it's not time for a feed.

- Visit a care provider

If you want to stick it out you can always go to a medical professional. Maybe you are going through a hormonal imbalance and you need to be checked out. Psychiatry consultants can help you change your perceptions about life and teach you coping mechanisms to help you through this difficult time.

- Talk to someone about it

You need to talk to your close friends, therapists, and other experts to seek support. By talking to someone, you will be encouraged that you're not alone. Look online for motivational speakers who can give you motivations for your life and show you how to stay positive.

WHY BREASTFEEDING DOESN'T GO WELL EVERY TIME

*E*very mama dreams about the moment she'll begin to hold her small ones in her arms, take care of them, and start providing their most essential needs. Most mamas know that milk is the basic need for every newborn baby. She wishes to feed the most nutritious thing to her child.

As mamas, most women know that breastmilk is the best option for their infants. However, for a few breastfeeding mamas, this desire may become a source of stress and unease if their milk supply is not enough after delivery. These kinds of thoughts make them worry.

During and after pregnancy, there are so many myths that every mama has heard about. She'll have many questions. Why am I not able to breastfeed? Is it normal if I don't breastfeed my baby? Will it cause a problem between me and my child if I don't give him my milk? If these are problems, then how would I get rid of the issues?

For mamas who are stressing about not producing enough milk for their child, then let me tell you that this happens with several moms. It's genuine that a few ladies are incapable of breastfeeding at all. A few ladies produce a low supply of breast-milk. Such ladies often feel completely helpless and alone. If this is you, be kind to yourself. You have not done anything wrong.

You're not alone – several mamas face such problems. According to Canadian and US overviews, it appears that 11 to 31% of moms never start breastfeeding, and 4% stop within the primary (first) phase of childbirth. An extra 15% of moms stop nursing before their child is 2 months old. Luckily, there are other safe, nutritious substitutes for human milk and many, many babies have survived and thrived on them.

If not breastmilk, then what should you feed your child? Many kinds of formula milk are available in the market but of course, most mamas have many questions in their minds. So, their first instinct is to do away with the thing making them unable to breastfeed. Some of the problems can be resolved but some cannot. If the cause cannot be resolved then there are other options to pick. But first, mama must know the reason.

DOES BREASTFEEDING WORK EVERY TIME?

Let me be honest, breastfeeding can be difficult and doesn't work every time. Breasts are sensitive organs that don't always work as we are expecting them to. You probably expect and hope that you will be able to breastfeed your infant, even if it takes several attempts. The reality is that for diverse reasons, a few mamas are incapable of breastfeeding. It can be very painful to discover that you can't breastfeed. So, what should you do if you find yourself in that situation? There are some reasons why some mamas are not able to produce enough milk for their infants.

WHAT KEEPS YOU FROM BEING ABLE TO BREASTFEED?

There are several reasons why some mamas may not be able to breastfeed their infants. A few cannot deliver a sufficient breastmilk supply, while others may have to take certain medicines or undergo treatments that are not safe for breastfeeding. Also, some medical conditions are not appropriate for breastfeeding. In many conditions, the mama may have to pump and give the baby the breastmilk from a bottle, or they may have to pause breastfeeding for some time and then start again. Some reasons for not being able to breastfeed are:

1. Low supply of breastmilk

Most new mamas stress that they may not be able to produce an adequate amount of milk for their babies. However, an unsolvable low breastmilk supply is rare and it is mostly the result of basic conditions. With treatment, a few issues can be remedied but there are a few issues that may never be helped. These include:

- Polycystic ovary syndrome (PCOS)
- Hypothyroidism
- Breast surgery
- Treatments for breast cancer (chemotherapy and radiation)
- Insufficient glandular tissue in the breasts (note that this has nothing to do with the size of your breasts)

ADDITIONALLY, variables like premature birth, maternal weight, high blood pressure, and diabetes may also affect milk supply.

If you have a low breastmilk supply from these causes, you will not be able to breastfeed exclusively. Supplementing with newborn child formula or benefactor milk is nothing to be embarrassed about. You are helping your baby to meet his nutritional needs, which is exactly what a good mama does.

1. Postpartum depression

Postpartum depression is connected to chemical, social, and mental changes that happen after having a baby. The term covers a range of physical and emotional changes that many new moms encounter. This depression can be treated with pharmaceuticals and counseling.

Your body goes through a lot of changes during and after pregnancy. Sometimes during or after pregnancy, it is okay if you feel a lack of emotions, devastated and sad, but if it continues for more than two weeks, you should seek help.

The period of pregnancy and a few weeks after giving birth makes a woman more susceptible to depression. There are tremendous emotional, economic, physical, and social changes during this time. Some women may be at risk of falling into serious mental problems including intense depression and anxiety which make it extremely difficult to breastfeed.

I will discuss more about postpartum depression in later chapters.

1. Mama is a drug addict

THE BABY'S health is and welfare is vital and his health is closely tied to his mama's milk. If she is a drug addict who is consuming things like cocaine, heroin, and alcohol then her milk will be harmful to her child. These substances are transferred to a baby in breastmilk. Of course, this is injurious to the baby's development. Such mamas are not recommended to give their breastmilk to their babies. However, if the mom wants to breastfeed, then she needs to stop taking drugs completely.

REASONS THE BABY REFUSES TO BREASTFEED

The breastfeeding relationship between the mama and the child is ongoing. Every day you experience new things and those things keep on changing. Sometimes when you think that you have everything under control, the baby comes up with something new that changes things and brings new challenges for you.

You may be happy that you have established a well-managed breastfeeding routine but suddenly, your baby refuses to breastfeed. You may be left wondering, *Oh Lord! What is happening? Why is he not willing to breastfeed anymore?*

My dear, you are not the only one – most moms go through this. I also experienced this and it took me many days to figure out why my baby was refusing to nurse. I figured it out and I'm here to gladly share my experiences with you so that you won't have to suffer for days.

There can be a lot of factors causing this and they can be from the mama's side as well as from the baby's. Let us discuss some of them and I'll share their solutions with you.

- Change in smell and taste of breastmilk

Sometimes your meals and drinks can alter the taste and smell of your breastmilk. The taste and smell of many things you eat can be reflected in your breastmilk. For example, if you eat a highly spiced curry. The taste and smell of your breastmilk can hinder the breastfeeding process.

The baby can get a distinct taste of certain flavors in your breastmilk far ahead in the day. In some cases, the foods you are eating, the drinks you are having, or certain medications and herbs you are consuming can change the taste of your breastmilk.

Generally, this is a good thing because it helps the baby to develop a wider palate for when you introduce table foods. However, if the taste or smell is too much, your baby may dislike your breastmilk. This is rare but it can be a cause of refusal of breastmilk by the baby.

Occasionally, something can affect the taste of your milk to a level where the baby thinks it is not breastmilk and he refuses it.

Both the smell of breastmilk and the smell of your breasts and body matter. Your breastmilk can be turned down by the baby if your breasts and body are smelling too strongly. This may happen with the use of strongly scented soaps, perfumes, or lotions.

Solutions

1. Go through your routine, checking things you are eating.
2. Make sure you are not using strongly scented perfumes.
3. Skip any meal or drink which has a strong flavor.
4. Think about any recent specific changes in your eating habits.
5. Check your medications to see whether they have a strong effect or smell.
6. Stop using scented soaps and lotions.
7. Stay clean and calm.

- The baby is experiencing some illness or discomfort

IF YOUR BABY is on a breastfeeding strike, it doesn't always mean that there is a problem with you or your milk. The baby may be suffering from some illness or discomfort.

Common illnesses can be a cold, bad throat, ear infection, stuffy nose, or stomach ailment. These cause pain and breathing problems for the baby while he tries to breastfeed. Sore cold and thrush can cause discomfort for the baby while breastfeeding.

In these situations, some babies will stop breastfeeding. Keep an eye on your baby's health issues and try to solve them as soon as possible so that your baby would have comfort in breastfeeding and stay healthy.

- Baby is distracted

MANY MOMS BREASTFEED their babies while watching TV or using mobiles or there is a lot of noise around them. It is a very common practice. Too many loud voices or sounds can distract your baby causing him to lose interest in breastfeeding or even refusing to breastfeed at all.

Sometimes moms start calling someone on phones while breastfeeding and this loud talking can distract the baby and he can refuse to breastfeed.

Try to avoid all these distractions while breastfeeding. Select a quiet place for breastfeeding with very few interruptions. Switch your phone to silent mode and turn the television or radio off. Try staring into your baby's eyes, smile, and talk quietly to him instead of using your mobile or watching TV. This will not only minimize the distractions but also will increase your bonding with the baby.

If you feel bored in silent places, turn on some soothing music which will make you and your baby feel relaxed.

- The baby is sleepy

NEWBORNS ONLY HAVE two things to do – feed and sleep. They need proper sleep to grow. However, if your baby is feeling more sleepy than normal, he may refuse to breastfeed.

Babies can feel sleepy due to many reasons. Maybe some of your medications, which can pass through into the breastmilk, are making him sleepy. Or the baby might be too weak or unhealthy to stay active and awake. Premature babies are often very sleepy and need to be woken up for feeding.

This sleepiness is temporary. Just change the baby's sleep routines and try to keep him active during the times he should be awake. Check that any medication you're on is compatible with breastfeeding and have him checked by a doctor if he's sick.

- Baby is teething

TEETHING IS A VERY painful and difficult process for young ones because it causes huge discomfort or even. Teething is a process in which a baby is growing his new teeth. Teeth erupt and emerge through the gums, irritating them and making them inflamed.

This irritation and pain can be the reason for the baby's refusal of breastmilk. Babies will not be comfortable breastfeeding during teething days and you may not know right away. Sucking may cause gums soreness.

You should try to soothe your baby's gums. Medications may be prescribed to help the process. Also, you could get a teething toy that will help soothe him in between feeds.

- Some other common reasons for breastfeeding refusal

HERE'S a list of other reasons why a baby can refuse to breastfeed:

- Recent immunization
- Baby refusing one breast (try the second breast if baby refuses one)
- Baby confused by bottle-feeding
- Biting
- Weaning
- Hormonal changes in the mama (can affect milk production)

HOW TO STOP BREASTMILK REFUSAL

Fortunately, there are tons of solutions and hacks that you can apply to get your baby out of breastmilk refusal. I've already discussed some of them at the start of this chapter, but now we'll summarize them.

Minimize distractions

CHOOSE A QUIET, peaceful place for breastfeeding. If possible, select a part of the house where there is very little noise and you and your baby feel comfortable. You may dim the lights to provide a soothing and satisfying atmosphere for you and the baby.

If guests are coming, make sure you manage to breastfeed in a quiet place where the baby can't hear chattering people and stay relaxed. Your bedroom is probably a good option if you have a comfortable chair in there. If not, try propping yourself up on the bed with pillows.

Make sure the volume of TV or music is at its minimum level to decrease the distraction.

Try changing positions

IF YOUR BABY is refusing to breastfeed and there's no obvious reason for it, try changing breastfeeding positions. You can switch from a cradle to a lying down position in which your baby will feel more relaxed and may start feeding.

Find out changes in your routine

THINK through your routine to look for any changes. Think about what you have eaten or drank in the last few days that may have affected the taste or smell of your breastmilk. Check out the medications you have taken as they may have caused this.

Try changing your soap or body lotion if they have a strong fragrance. Try changing the deodorant you are using. The strong smell of all these can be a reason for the breastfeeding strike.

Are you stressed about something? If *yes*, this can affect your milk production and breastfeeding routine. Try relaxing and sorting out any issues which are causing stress.

Check out if you are maybe pregnant with the next baby. This also affects milk production, the taste of your milk and also brings some physical changes.

Consult someone

.   .   .

IF THE BREASTFEEDING strike has been prolonged, you need to see a breastfeeding specialist and get help. You should also visit a consultant pediatrician to find out about the health of your baby.

Alternatives are a breastfeeding club or group in your area that may be able to help.

You can also try cup feeding, finger feeding, or breastfeeding supplementer devices.

Try breast pumping if you are getting low on milk production as this will increase your milk production. Try giving hand expressed milk to your baby with a spoon or bottle to redevelop his taste for your milk. You can then try breastfeeding again.

Some other solutions you can try:

- Using your hand, express a few drops of your milk into your baby's mouth to give him a taste.
- Try singing gentle poems or songs to your baby while breastfeeding.
- Nurse while walking around the house.
- Stimulate your let-down reflex by taking a warm shower before you feed the baby or sipping on a warm beverage.

MEDICAL AND PHYSICAL REASONS THAT CAUSE LOW BREASTMILK SUPPLY

When breastfeeding, if your baby is not gaining weight, it may become a source of tension for you. You may start thinking about whether you are producing enough milk for your baby or not. Sometimes it's just is a natural event that you are producing little or no milk. But we have to keep in view that some medical reasons cause this situation.

Here are a few of the common reasons for low milk supply and a few measures that may help you out.

- IGT - Insufficient Glandular Tissue (Hypoplasia)

Everyone knows that breastfeeding comes naturally. Some mamas can produce adequate milk supplies for their babies but in many cases, some mamas are just not able to breastfeed.

Some women's breasts don't grow normally for various reasons. IGT is a very rare condition that can be a reason for low or no breastmilk production. The mama may not have sufficient milk-making ducts to fulfill their child's milk needs. Ducts develop through each pregnancy and breastfeeding invigorates the development of more ducts and tissues. So, this may be less of an issue if it's your second or third child.

Signs of Hypoplasia

1. Small, widely-spaced breasts
2. Areolas (dark area around the nipples) seem to be swollen
3. Uneven-sized breasts
4. The breasts did not increase in size during the pregnancy

- Contraindicated medications

NUMEROUS MEDICATIONS, including those which need a doctor's prescription, are agreeable with breastfeeding, but a few are not.

Some medicines are completely incompatible with breastfeeding. These include:

1. Radioactive iodine
2. Some sedatives
3. Medicines that cause drowsiness
4. Medicines that suppress breathing
5. Antiretroviral drugs (for HIV)

- Breast surgeries

If you have had any sort of past breast surgery, including biopsies, breast reduction, or breast augmentation, you may have a low milk supply. Because these are natural organs the surgeries may generate such problems. In the case of mamas who have had breast reductions, they may have lost many milk ducts. This will probably make breastfeeding a challenging task. The other surgeries may also have caused damage to the milk-producing parts.

- Hormonal complications

Mamas who have polycystic ovary syndrome (PCOS), diabetes, high blood pressure, or hormonal issues that made it troublesome for them to conceive may experience difficulties with breastfeeding. Any of these problems may affect the production of milk since the ability to produce milk relies on the hormonal signs that get sent to the breasts.

- Hormonal birth control

During breastfeeding, some mamas do not want to get pregnant again so they use birth control pills. These pills may not affect the milk production of some mamas. However, a few mamas face the problem of low milk production. To improve the production, first, you will need to stop taking the hormones and switch to another birth control method. If still there is no improvement after coming off the pills, go and talk to your physician.

- Jaundice

Jaundice in the first week of life is normal in newborn babies, especially if they are small or premature. Jaundice will make your infant sleepier than normal so that he keeps on sleeping and does not wake up for breastfeeding as frequently as he should. In this case, you will need to pump up your milk to keep up the supply otherwise later, it can cause a low milk supply for your baby. Remember that it's important to feed your newborn frequently when they have jaundice even if you have to wake him up. This helps to flush the yellow color through his system. Once the jaundice is better, he will likely start breastfeeding well, and then you might decrease or stop the pumping.

- Inverted nipples

When nipples are inverted, they appear flat against the areola (dark area around nipples) and look like they go inwards rather than sticking out. Another term used for inverted nipples is *retracted nipples*. Some mamas have inverted nipples since they were born and some get them later in life.

This kind of nipples can be found both in males and females but they are more of a problem for females because they may find it difficult or in some cases can't breastfeed. Sometimes, there is only one inverted nipple, and sometimes both.

- Active tuberculosis (TB)

Tuberculosis (TB) is a serious disease that affects the lungs and is spread through the air by infected people coughing. It is very infectious, so healthcare specialists say that moms with active TB don't breastfeed their newborn child, since a mama may unintentionally transfer germs to her infant by sneezing, coughing, or breathing on him. So, a mama with infectious TB may pump her breast and give extracted milk to her infant in bottles. The TB medication passes into the milk in very small quantities only and does not seem to harm the baby.

- HIV

HIV is a disease that can be transmitted from person to person by bodily fluids. A mama with this disease can transfer the virus to her child through breastfeeding. HIV is passed on via the breastmilk so mamas are not allowed to feed their babies with their milk. The mamas are recommended to give a substitute such as formula milk or donor milk from milk banks.

- Mamas with breast cancer

If a mama is diagnosed with breast cancer during nursing, most physicians will recommend that she should not continue breastfeeding. Many treatments used for breast cancer can be passed to the infant via the breastmilk, including hormone therapies and chemotherapy drugs. Stopping breastfeeding can even lower the blood supply to the breasts, making them smaller and easier for the doctors to examine, and much less likely to become diseased.

SOME BARRIERS TO BREASTFEEDING

Breastfeeding is vital but some issues cause mamas to stop breastfeeding their babies. Some of these issues are faced by almost every mama. Here are some of the most common deal breakers:

- Mama needs to go to the office

When mama needs to go back to work, she may prefer to give formula milk to her baby. If not formula milk, then she pumps her breasts and extracts milk into bottles before leaving for work. Some workplaces do not allow mamas to breastfeed there so they hand over their babies to caretakers. Some workplaces have different policies and time frames and even provide breastfeeding facilities.

- Breastfeeding in public

Many women feel embarrassed to breastfeed in public, or even feel shy, especially a first-time mama who has recently given birth. There are also very few breastfeeding facilities for mamas in public spaces, so they avoid breastfeeding their babies in public places.

- Promotion of formula milk

TECHNOLOGY HAS BECOME SO vast that the ads and promotions of brands can affect the mindsets of mamas, leading them to believe that formula feeding is better and more convenient. Some mamas, after watching promotional ads of formula milk think that it is comparable to breastmilk and they start feeding their babies with it.

WHAT TO DO IF YOU HAVE A LOW MILK SUPPLY

If you believe that your baby is not obtaining sufficient milk, see a lactation consultant or breastfeeding professional. They'll tell you if you have a low milk supply and watch you while breast-feeding to make sure your child is latching on properly and getting adequate milk. The most important principle is that the more your baby suckles, the more milk you will produce to keep up with the demand. This is why you should feed the baby often if your supply is low. Use a breast pump after feeds to completely empty the breasts and stimulate milk production. This milk can be frozen for times when you just don't have enough milk.

Furthermore, you can attempt to have a lot of "skin-to-skin" contact with your baby before and during feeds to energize the hormone oxytocin which gets your breastmilk flowing. You can also use a relaxation method, like playing your favorite calming music, to cut back on any kind of depression or sadness that might be affecting your milk supply.

With support, most mamas with low milk production can successfully breastfeed their children, and a few can make a full milk supply.

BREAST PUMPS AND EXCLUSIVE PUMPING?

a breast pump is a device that lactating mothers use to take out milk from their breasts. It may be a hand or foot-operated device or the device may be electrical.

Breast pumps are used for several reasons. Many mothers use breast pumps to continue breastfeeding when they go back to their workplace. They extract their milk at work which is then later fed to their babies by their caretakers with bottles.

A breast pump may also be used to improve lactation for mothers who have a low milk supply.

Additionally, a breast pump is used to assist with a range of challenges mothers may face when breastfeeding, including difficulties in latching, separation from a baby during medical aid, feeding a child who cannot take out the milk from the mother's breast by himself, and relieving breast engorgement (a condition where the mother's breasts are overfull from milk and causing pain).

Some children are unable to breastfeed from birth. There may be several reasons for this. The child may be premature (born before time) or have other special needs such as a cleft lip and palate. You will then need to use a breast pump and extract milk.

Some moms use a breast pump if they need milk for mixing with the baby's solid food (After 6 months of age). Another use for the breast pump is to extract breastmilk for donations. Donor milk is on the market from milk banks for babies who for various reasons cannot have their own mother's milk.

Breast pumps, like bras, come with different-sized cups. Before buying a breast pump, choose the size that is right for you, making sure it's not too small or too big. Choosing a pump that is your size will make it difficult to use and may hurt your breasts.

TYPES OF BREAST PUMPS

Breast pumps usually consist of a suction cup (that is fitted to the mother's nipple), funnel, and a milk collection bottle. The pump plays the role of your baby and sucks milk from your breasts. The extracted breastmilk flows through a funnel and is collected in the bottle. All the parts of a pump which come into contact with the milk must be sterilized.

Two types of breast pumps we will look at are:

- Manual breast pumps

In this kind of breast pump, an individual is asked to continuously press a handle to get milk. Manual pumps are best for short-term usage. These are small and not too costly. The manual pump requires an individual to do the work so it can be tiring to use.

- Electric breast pumps

Electric breast pumps are power-driven by a motor that delivers suction with the aid of a plastic cup that is placed over the nipples. If you are planning to use pumps regularly and for the long term, then do consider buying an electric pump. This pump works faster than a manual one and your energy is not required. Additionally, you can extract milk from both breasts at the same time. Hospital-grade breast pumps are also electric but are designed for multiple users.

EXCLUSIVE PUMPING

Perhaps you accept that mother's milk is the leading food choice for your baby, but for some reason, you are not able to breast-feed. What can you do in such a situation? That's the situation where exclusive pumping is ideal. Exclusive pumping is a way to supply your child with your breastmilk without putting him to the breast.

Exclusive pumping is also known as *EPing* or *breastmilk feedings*. It is the method of expelling the breastmilk from your breasts at fixed times all through the day. Then you will be able to give the breastmilk to your child either by using a bottle or some other feeding strategy.

The word "exclusive pumping" indicates that the baby **is not nursed at all but is still fed with breastmilk.** Exclusive pumping is the second-best option next to breastfeeding for feeding your child.

Exclusive pumping can be time-consuming and tiring, particularly if you need to pump for a long period. However, the longer you can give your child your breastmilk, the better it will be for them.

REASONS FOR EXCLUSIVE PUMPING

The mother may decide whether to exclusively pump or breast-feed her child. There are various reasons many mothers choose exclusive pumping.

- The baby is premature and cannot breastfeed
- The baby has difficulties with latching onto the breast properly
- The mother has pain while breastfeeding but tolerates pumping
- The mother thinks she has a low milk supply so uses this method to keep checking whether her baby is getting enough milk or not
- The mother needs to return to work
- The baby refuses to breastfeed directly
- The baby now has teeth and causes pain when he bites the nipple

HOW FREQUENTLY TO PUMP

A newborn will take a small bottle of breastmilk every 2 to 3 hours. So, in the first few weeks, you ought to attempt to pump at least every 2 to 3 hours to encourage your body to generate a healthy milk supply.

As your baby grows older, he will take more at each feeding but the time between each feed should increase. As long as your milk supply is good, you will be able to extend the time between pumping sessions as well.

HOW LONG TO PUMP AT EACH SESSION?

At each session, you need to pump for at least 15 minutes on each side. It might take several minutes for your milk to let down, so you need to give yourself sufficient time. Moreover, you need to try to completely empty your breasts since this is what stimulates your breasts to produce more milk.

After you clear out your breasts and no more milk is streaming into the container, continue to pump for 1 to 5 minutes longer to stimulate milk production.

BREASTMILK BANKS

breastmilk provides all the nourishment a child needs in the first six months. Mother donor milk from a milk bank could be a good alternative if a child cannot obtain it straight from the source. If you are considering using donor milk, it is important to know the advantages and hazards first.

breastmilk contains nourishment that is basic for a baby's development especially for those born prematurely. When the infant cannot be breastfed by his mom, sanitized human donor milk from milk banks is the next best option.

If the mother is producing a low or no milk supply for her baby and she doesn't want to give him formula milk, then the best option is for her to get donor milk from breastmilk banks. In this way, her baby will get all the nourishment that breastmilk contains and avoid the disadvantages of bottle feeding.

Generally, breastfeeding mothers extract breastmilk, freeze it and then give it to milk banks. The milk banks provide them with cleaned, sterilized collection bottles, name labels, and breast pumps and will give instructions to the mothers about how to transport and store the breastmilk securely. The milk bank then purifies the milk to kill any germs. Milk banks do not give any rewards to the donors.

IS DONATED MILK SAFE?

When it comes to donor milk, every mother wants to know if it's safe. Generally, it is safe. This milk is donated by mothers who produce more milk than their own babies can use. Before donating milk, each mother is tested for various illnesses. The milk is sterilized by the banks so it is not harmful to babies.

WHO CAN DONATE BREASTMILK?

Not all mothers can donate breastmilk because some may have infections or other medical issues. When they have such issues, their milk may not be healthy for infants.

When a mother wants to donate milk, the bank will require her to go through a screening process for germs that will pass into her milk.

The staff at the bank will also want to know if she is in a healthy condition and if she takes any medicines on a daily basis. They will also inquire if a mother takes any kind of drugs. Milk bank staff will only take donated milk if the mother is healthy and her milk is secure for the babies who will receive it.

POSTPARTUM DEPRESSION

$\mathcal{B}$ecoming a mama is a happy and blessed occasion for most women. Nothing can make her happier than having a little soul in her arms. Sometimes though, this joy is converted into sadness and anxiety that lead to serious depression. This can happen for many different medical and physical reasons.

Postpartum depression is connected to chemical, social, and mental changes that happen when a woman has a baby or is breastfeeding. The term represents a variety of physical and psychological changes that several moms encounter. This depression can be helped with pharmaceuticals and other forms of therapy.

Your body goes through a lot of changes during and after pregnancy. At these times, it is normal to experience a lack of emotions or feel tired, sad, and low, but if it continues for more than two weeks, you should get help.

If ignored, such issues can lead to full-blown depression in which you will not feel love and affection towards your newborn baby. This is called postpartum depression. Post-partum means "period after childbirth", the period in which you start breastfeeding. Many mamas get baby blues within the first few days of mama-hood but if it continues it can become a very serious but treatable medical issue found in one out of seven mamas.

The period of pregnancy and a few weeks after giving birth makes a woman more susceptible to emotional lows. Every mama goes through emotional, economic, physical, and social changes during this time. Some of them may be at risk of falling into serious mental problems consisting of intense depression and anxiety.

Baby blues is a condition of a very short period of emotional drought a new mama can feel right after giving birth. It usually doesn't interfere with normal activities of life. It may trigger symptoms like crying for no reason, agitation, depression, and anxiety. These symptoms should go away in a week or two, but if they last longer, you may be edging towards postpartum depression.

Don't confuse baby blues with postpartum depression. Baby blues go away in 10-15 days but postpartum depression can continue for weeks or months and it should be treated as soon as possible for the sake of both mama and child.

SYMPTOMS OF POSTPARTUM DEPRESSION

Postpartum depression is a combination of physical, mental, and emotional symptoms. These can appear during pregnancy or after the birth. Sometimes these are very difficult to detect. These can include:

- Sadness and crying for no reason
- Constant depressed mood
- Loss of enjoyment in things enjoyed before childbirth
- Sleeping too much
- Insomnia
- Fatigued body and low energy levels
- Increase in unnecessary activities like not sitting still,
- Trouble with speaking or writing
- Feelings of inadequacy
- Feelings of intense guilt
- Inability to make decisions and think clearly
- Thinking of death and suicide
- Not feeling affection or love towards your baby
- Feeling extreme nervousness around baby
- Blaming yourself for not being a good mom
- Thoughts of harming the baby or yourself
- Strong anger
- Feeling hungry all the time or eating nothing for hours
- Panic attacks

A mama who is going through postpartum depression may have a few of these symptoms and some of them might be very intense. This may cause her to feel alone, embarrassed, and humiliated.

Although there is no diagnostic test for evaluating this depression, it is a very medical illness and should be taken seriously. Any mama feeling any of these symptoms strongly should consult a medical professional. If you only have one or two of the symptoms listed above and they are not getting worse, you may not have postpartum depression.

WHICH MAMAS ARE AT RISK OF POSTPARTUM DEPRESSION?

Any new mama or pregnant woman can get symptoms of this depression or other mood disorder. Women who have a family history of mood disorders are more susceptible to falling into postpartum depression.

Women who are going through other crises such as financial or marriage difficulties while pregnant or new mamas can easily fall into this form of depression. Also, those who don't have a support network.

Breastfeeding struggles can also trigger this depression if a mama cannot cope with breastfeeding and finds herself in a difficult position. She starts thinking of herself as not worthy of her child if she cannot even breastfeed him.

Changes in sexual and work relationships, hormone levels, or worrying too much about parenting (maybe due to financial changes) can also trigger this depression. Lack of sleep during pregnancy or early days of mama-hood is another cause.

Fathers can also get symptoms of postpartum depression, especially ones with a previous history of depression and mental illness. Young fathers can fall into depression in the first year of childbirth due to mental, physical, or financial stress.

CAUSES OF POSTPARTUM DEPRESSION

If you have postpartum depression, it doesn't mean you had done something wrong and caused it to happen. As we've seen, there can be many things that cause the onset of this depression and they are not the same for every mama. Some common causes of postpartum depression include:

- Previous history of stress and deep depression
- Breastfeeding struggles are out of hand
- Breastfeeding not going well
- Stressful or devastating event during pregnancy
- Age of the mama (younger moms are more vulnerable)
- Uncertainty about being pregnant
- Children (the more you have, the greater the risk)
- Inheritance of mood disorders
- Experiencing a great loss during pregnancy
- Giving birth to an abnormal child
- Giving birth to twins or triplets
- Having PMDD (premenstrual dysphoric disorder)
- Marital struggles

There is often not a single cause of postpartum depression but sometimes many different social, emotional, mental, and physical problems combine to trigger it. Some of the following issues may also contribute to this depression:

Lack of sleep

MAMAS SOMETIMES ARE KEPT AWAKE all night due to feeding sessions or a crying baby. If this isn't addressed, they can become sleep-deprived. Being sleepless or suffering from intense insomnia before or after pregnancy can be a cause of postpartum depression. Lack of sleep makes a person emotionally and physically sick and she will become distressed even when dealing with insignificant problems.

Sleeplessness leads to deep stress on both the mind and body of the person. A person with very little or no sleep is more susceptible to falling into physical and mental disorders, especially stress and anxiety.

Anxiety

FROM THE VERY FIRST day they find out they're pregnant, many mamas become anxious about whether they have the ability to take care of a baby. They start worrying about it and start questioning whether they will be a good mom.

After giving birth, some women start worrying about breastfeeding and take it as a challenge. If she somehow can't manage to breastfeed her baby properly, she might get stressed about it.

Some pregnant women worry about their capability of giving birth. They fear that their bodies might not be strong enough to give birth to a baby. If they have to have a Cesarean section, some women start thinking of themselves as underrated females who cannot even give birth to their children the proper way.

This anxiety can lead to prolonged depression and can be a cause of postpartum depression.

Hormones

THERE ARE a series of prominent changes in hormones both during and after pregnancy. Hormone levels fluctuate according to the pregnancy or postpartum period the Mama is in. These hormones are not only related to the tasks of pregnancy or giving birth but they also influence your emotional, physical, and mental state.

A sudden drop in some hormones can trigger stress and play a role in creating this depression. For example, estrogen and progesterone levels drop drastically when you give birth to the baby. This can contribute to symptoms of postpartum depression.

Some other hormones which are produced by the thyroid gland may also go down quickly and cause stress, sadness, or sluggishness.

Self-image

MANY EVENTS CONTRIBUTE to creating our self-image. Sometimes, due to major changes after having a baby and various struggles, you may consider yourself of low value. You may feel less attractive than before and feel like you have no control over your life.

A mama can create her own bad self-image when she fails in breastfeeding. She starts thinking of herself as a failure and believes that she is not a good mama.

This negative self-image can also contribute to pushing you into postpartum depression.

TYPES/STAGES OF POSTPARTUM DEPRESSION

Postpartum depression can be of different stages depending upon its severity and time. It can be mild to severe.

- Mild – baby blues

Almost 70 % of all mamas fell into baby blues within the first week after giving birth to their babies. They may feel rapid mood changes like feeling extremely happy at one moment and feeling extremely unhappy at the next moment. They may start crying without any reason and continue for minutes and hours.

They can feel annoyed, bad-tempered, isolated, edgy, nervous, grieved, or a failure.

The baby blues may last for a few hours or 10-15 days after giving birth. This condition does not need medical treatment. Women who are struggling can join support groups for new mamas or can talk to other mamas about it.

However, if baby blues are prolonged, they may get severe and cause depression.

- Moderate – postpartum depression

Starting feelings of depression can be similar to baby blues but this time they will come strongly and continue beyond the first two weeks after giving birth. This depression can happen within a few days of delivery or after a few months. It can happen while giving birth to any baby, not necessarily the first one.

Women experiencing postpartum depression often change their daily routines. They stop doing their everyday chores – sometimes even the ones which include taking care of the baby. Their mood changes become intense and they start losing feelings of affection and love for their babies.

This condition needs to be immediately reported to medical professionals and should be treated on a serious note. If left untreated it becomes devastating for both mama and baby. Although it is a serious condition, it can be treated with medication and therapies.

- Severe – postpartum psychosis

WHEN POSTPARTUM DEPRESSION becomes severe and is left untreated, it can change into a horrifying condition called postpartum psychosis. This is a serious mental illness. Mamas suffering from it start:

- Losing touch with reality
- Hearing sounds and things that are not really happening (auditory hallucinations)
- Having misconceptions
- Seeing things that are not there (visual hallucinations)
- Experiencing severe insomnia
- Feeling angry and restless

Women who suffer from postpartum psychosis need medical attention right away. Almost every case needs to be treated with medications. In some cases, hospitalization becomes necessary because the mama can be at risk of hurting herself or her baby.

TREATMENT OF POSTPARTUM DEPRESSION

Many mamas keep suffering in silence and they just take these symptoms as normal struggles of pregnancy and childbirth. They fail to get medical attention. Most symptoms of stress and depression start during the pregnancy so treatment should start right away.

Awareness and understanding of everything can lead to healthy childbirth and a happy postpartum time. Like other types of depression, postpartum depression can also be treated by talk therapy (psychotherapy), medication, self-improvement, and support. Usually, these methods are combined to produce a well-rounded treatment and good results.

Let us discuss in more detail all the possible ways to treat postpartum depression.

Medication

IF THE POSTPARTUM depression is mild, medication should not be the first-line treatment but if it is severe, then medication is the first choice to go with. Most medication has side effects for mamas so they need to be checked properly before being taken and side effects should be reported immediately.

Before starting the medications, doctors do a risk-benefit ratio analysis. It will clarify whether the medication is the right option for a particular mama or not. There are several medications that can be used to treat this depression and all of them need a prescription and dosage chart from a medical specialist.

Most antidepressants are used to treat all types of depression and stress, including postpartum depression. Antidepressants may have greater side effects than other medications, so they should be used more cautiously. These side effects may include weakness, tiredness, decrease in sex drive, faintness, etc.

These medications don't start giving results right away and sometimes need to be taken for a while before an improvement is seen.

Some antidepressants are safe to take while breastfeeding and some are not. This is why you need to get your doctor's advice and prescription before taking them. Never use any that have been given to you by a friend as they may not be safe when breastfeeding.

Similarly, if you start getting symptoms of depression while pregnant, you should get medical care. Many antidepressants are considered safe for pregnant women and can prevent them from falling into postpartum depression. Proper awareness, medications, and consulting can prevent you from getting post-partum depression even if you have symptoms in pregnancy. Common antidepressants used during pregnancy are:

- SSRIs (Selective serotonin reuptake inhibitors) – may have side effects and can cause lung damage in newborns
- SNRIs (Serotonin and norepinephrine reuptake inhibitors)
- Wellbutrin (Bupropion)
- TCAs (Tricyclic antidepressants)

The following antidepressants are given to treat postpartum depression:

- The most widely used and recently discovered is Brexanolone (Zulresso). It's approved by the FDA and is recognized as good in this situation. It may not be safe during breastfeeding.
- Esketamine – is also one of the most widely prescribed medicines for postpartum depression. It's not safe in pregnancy. Given as a nasal spray.

These medications have some prompt and strong effects right after they are administered. So in almost every case, they are given to the patient in a doctor's clinic or some medical facility under the control of doctors and nurses.

Psychotherapy

POSTPARTUM DEPRESSION IS ALSO TREATED with psychotherapy i.e. speech therapy. A medical consultant or a psychologist gives the patient therapy sessions in which he talks about her depression and listens to her thoughts. Then he suggests some strategies for the mama to work on. The therapist also helps the woman to get rid of her fears, sadness, and illusions by talking to her and giving her hope sessions.

These therapies are just like normal psychiatric sessions attended for any form of stress or depression. Mama will learn to control her emotions such as anger and she'll know her worth. These therapies are of great help and they result in very positive changes in patients and often help them feel normal again.

Hormone Therapy

IF THE LEVEL of hormones such as estrogen fall to a drastically low level, hormonal therapy is given to the affected mama to maintain a hormonal balance.

Sometimes hormone therapy can have side effects like:

- Vomiting
- In most severe cases, certain cancers
- Weight loss or gain

HOW TO DEAL WITH POSTPARTUM DEPRESSION

After consulting a medical professional and starting medication or therapy, there are few other things you can do by yourself to improve your condition.

Communicate

· · ·

IF YOU ARE a reserved person by nature, you'll keep things to yourself and lack the courage to express them. It is very helpful to talk during a depression. You should share everything with someone you trust such as your partner. This will give you a sense that you are not alone in life and others are here to listen to whatever you say. This will improve your condition.

Try to get away from isolation

ISOLATION IS a bad thing for depression and it's one of the main causes of it. Try to remain in touch with close friends and family members. It is not about becoming a social icon but just having a few good hours and relaxing with people you like.

Seek out a support group for depression sufferers particularly linked to new moms. You may make some new friends and will feel less alone by connecting with others in the same situation. If you previously were a member of a social group like a book club, rejoin them. Being in a group helps you focus on normal things other than depression and child care.

Cut back on responsibilities

YOU MAY NOT BE able to take on the same number of responsibilities as before. Cut out the non-essential things and focus on what's most important only. Focus on taking care of yourself and your baby and nurturing your relationship with your partner. Leave things like keeping a perfect house and garden and entertaining friends for a later time. Spend more time relaxing and playing with your baby.

Relax and rest

. . .

THIS IS the most vital thing for a mom having postpartum depression. You need to stay relaxed and rest properly. Try to have proper sleep hours and rest in a quiet place. Do not exhaust yourself with heavy work or tasks that stress you.

Meditation and massages can also help you to relax.

SNS FEEDING

*S*NS stands for **"SUPPLEMENTAL NURSING SYSTEM"**. This is the most important technique which is used to give supplemental feeds to babies during breastfeeding. This system forms an exclusive and affectionate relationship between a mama and her baby. It inspires both of them to keep going on the journey of breastfeeding. This system is all about giving any extra milk or supplements to the baby along with breastfeeding.

When breastfeeding is not working for you and your baby, it is recommended to use tube feeding along with breastfeeding. The best tube feeding technique is SNS feeding. There can be many reasons for low breastmilk supply and the baby will stay weak and not gain sufficient weight if the supply isn't supplemented.

The extra nutrients and supplements can be found in formula milk or donor milk. These supplements should be given with continued breastfeeding. SNS is there to provide you with such a system.

Traditionally, supplements are given by spoon, bottle, or syringe but the best option is SNS by which you will not lose the breast-feeding routine and the baby will still get supplements he needs for his good health.

Most mamas think of giving bottles to their babies for extra feeds, but SNS can be the best choice for supplementation especially for mamas who want to avoid nipple confusion and continue breastfeeding at the fullest.

WHAT IS SNS?

SNS is a tool that helps a breastfeeding mama to manage to give the supplements he needs while nursing him at the breast. With the help of this technique, a mama doesn't need to use a bottle or any other aid to provide her baby with supplements.

SNS consists of a feeder which is a very thin tube that is tucked inside the baby's mouth while he is latching onto the breast. One side of the tube is attached to the nipple of the breast and the other end is attached to a syringe full of pumped breastmilk or formula milk.

As the baby sucks the nipple, the tube attached to the nipple is also sucked and the plunger is pressed down which pushes milk through the tube into the baby's mouth.

Sometimes. one end of the tube is placed inside the bottle or syringe so when the baby sucks the other end of the tube it pulls milk up and it goes into the baby's mouth. But this requires more effort from the baby.

SNS FEEDING HELPED ME BOND WITH MY BABY AGAIN

The birth of my third baby had many complications and was the hardest time of life for me. I went through **breast reduction** and many other problems showed up at the same time including **Low milk supply**. I was greatly disturbed both physically and psychologically. Due to this, I was left with no option except to go for SNS tube feeding. I think it is the best option for mamas with a low milk supply.

Luckily, my baby girl was healthy when she was born. It was such a relief but suddenly due to complications, my breastmilk was not enough for my baby. She needed supplementation but I didn't want to use bottle feeding already in the first few weeks of childbirth. If I had done so, my baby may have stopped breastfeeding.

This was disturbing for me until I came to know about the Supplemental Nursing System feeding technique. This brought back hope in me and I was able to create a healthy breastfeeding routine with my baby girl. Most importantly, my baby was getting the supplements she needed.

This tool is very helpful for a lot of mamas like me with a low milk supply. I see it as life-saving. The SNS is designed to make mamas able to breastfeed when they are unable to do it. It also helps the baby to learn sucking behavior. For me, SNS had the following benefits:

- Great for moms who think they have a low breastmilk supply
- As the baby sucks on your breast, this tool helps mama's breasts to be stimulated for milk production

- It is the best tool for babies who need supplements in addition to mama's milk
- The baby learns to suck properly as it creates a vacuum-like mechanism at the breasts
- It helps mamas to get out of the psychological pressure and depression of not being able to breastfeed
- It helps mamas to get rid of the psychological tension of a low milk supply
- It helps in the development of affection and loving bond between mama and child

WHY USE SNS?

The SNS is usually used to supply supplemental milk to the baby while keeping him at the breast. There can be many reasons for using SNS:

- It is used for babies who are weak and need extra supplementation other the breastmilk.
- SNS is used for babies who have weak sucking reflexes or who are premature. This provides more milk to such babies in less time.
- Many mamas go through breast refusal and SNS can help them get it back because it helps in keeping the baby on the breast for longer.
- Some mamas have a low milk supply and they want to boost their lactation. SNS can help them as the baby sucks their breasts and they can be stimulated more.
- For adopted or surrogate babies, SNS can be used to give them a feeling of breastfeeding which will get them closer to you.
- In cases of nipple confusion and nipple preferences, SNS can help the baby to get back and stay on the breast for a longer time.

Some mamas need to adopt SNS for a short period. She may want to get his proper milk supply back by stimulating her breasts by the baby's sucking action. Some babies need supplemental milk for a short period and their mama adopts SNS feeding for a short period along with continued breastfeeding.

Some mamas have to adopt SNS feeding for a longer period because they are unable to produce sufficient milk for their baby and need some extra help. These mamas may have gone through breast surgery, breast reduction, or some other hormonal or physical reason that has affected their milk supply.

Adoptive mamas and those who used a surrogate for pregnancy also need a tube feeding system for their babies. Even a non-lactating mama can use the SNS system and mimic breastfeeding.

WHY SNS AND NOT BOTTLE FEEDING?

If a mama can give supplemental milk to her baby with a bottle, then why bother to use SNS? There are tons of reasons that clearly that SNS is a way better option than starting bottle feeding at an early age. SNS does the following:

- Decreases the risk of nipple confusion
- Increases milk supply of mother
- Decreases time of breastfeeding
- Helps mama to deal with her physical and hormonal aspects
- Decreases chances of breast refusal
- Increases bonding between mother and the baby

Few of these things cannot be achieved by bottle feeding. So, mamas, SNS is a very good option for supplementing your baby's feeds!

WHAT DO YOU NEED FOR SNS?

SNS is a simple setup and can easily be done by any mama. You just need to learn it once and you will be good to go afterward. First of all, you need to consult a breastfeeding specialist or lactation consultant who will guide you about which supplemental milk your baby needs and which tubes and containers you should use.

To prepare an SNS setup you'll need:

1. **A number 5 French feeding tube:** It is very cheap and is available in almost every medical store. Lactation consultants can also provide you with this.
2. **Container-like bottle:** This bottle will work as a reservoir for extra milk which can be pumped breastmilk, formula milk, or donor milk. A syringe can also be used for this purpose when mama wants to attach a milk container to her chest.
3. **Complete kit:** You can also buy a complete ready-made SNS kit which comes with everything – a syringe or small bottle, and a thin silicone tube that hangs around the mama's neck like a necklace.
4. **Medical tape:** You need medical tape to bind the end of the thin tube at your breast and nipple. This taping will help with a stable supply of milk from the container.
5. **Attachment ring**
6. **Valves:** These are used to control milk flow into a tube.

If a mom wants to do SNS feeding on a regular basis, I recommend that she buys a readymade kit. It is easier as you will not have to set it up by yourself. Another reason I'm recommending the SNS kit is that its tubes are easy to clean and can be sterilized easily.

HOW SNS WORKS

The tube and the SNS container are called **at-breast supplementer, nursing supplements, lactation aid,** or **artificial supply line.** One end of the tube is attached to the container of milk and the other end of the tube is taped at the breast and is attached just beside the nipple so that the baby must take the tube inside his mouth when he latches on.

Sometimes, the tube is not taped at the breast but is inserted into the corner of the baby's mouth. When the baby feeds on the breast, he also takes in the supplemented milk from the tube. As long as the baby keeps sucking the breast, the milk from the tube will flow into the baby's mouth.

It is just like sucking from a straw!

Some mamas use their fingers for tube feeding. Mama attaches the tube to her finger and puts it in the baby's mouth. When the baby starts sucking the finger, the milk comes from the tube into the baby's mouth by his sucking action. This type of tube feeding is only meant for a very short period. It may be for sucking training of the baby or teaching the baby how to latch on.

I tried introducing tube feeding to my baby when I was facing breast refusal due to low milk supply and it helped me get my baby back into the breastfeeding routine. We can help our babies to get back to latching on and training them to breast-feed with the help of SNS feeding.

CONTROLLING THE RATE OF MILK FLOW

Natural milk flow from mama's breast is very smooth and perfect but the flow of SNS feeding or bottle feeding always needed to be adjusted. Your baby needs the right speed of milk flow into his mouth so that he neither chokes with more milk nor has too small an amount of milk.

A low milk flow will not be managed by a baby who is weak and doesn't have proper sucking technique. When the supplementer is set at the right speed, your baby may get one swallow of milk flow with one suck or with 2-3 sucks in most of his feedings. The amount of milk flow from the tube differs with:

- **The position of the milk reservoir and baby:** The flow of the milk will be faster if the reservoir is placed at the level above the mouth of the baby and vice versa.
- **The diameter of the tube:** The narrower the tube, the slower will be the milk flow and vice versa. SNS feeding has several sizes of tubes so you can select the one you like.

If your baby is weak and he is a slow eater, you are recommended to use a wider tube so that your baby will get more milk faster. If your baby is growing well and eats well, you might go with a smaller tube. Most mamas, including me, go with medium-sized tubes.

If none of the tube sizes is working for your baby, you can tape two tubes of different sizes on one breast to increase milk flow. You can also tape one tube to the side of the reservoir with its open end facing upwards. This will create airflow into the reservoir more quickly and milk flow will increase. Milk leaves the reservoir when air enters it by sucking, so if the air enters quicker, the milk flow will automatically increase.

CLEANING THE SNS

When it comes to anything that is used for baby feeding, cleaning is the most important aspect. Germ-free feeding equipment is as necessary for your baby as his food. Cleaning the tubing system of SNS feeding is very important because germs can enter into a tube or reservoir if proper sterilization isn't done every time.

The tubes for SNS feeding are very narrow and small and they are difficult to clean. We have to change them regularly and use a new one. However, you can clean the reservoir with warm water or sterilize it with disinfectant.

ADVANTAGES OF SNS FEEDING

SNS feeding has a list of advantages I already shared with you but lets me summarize them here:

- Your baby easily gets some extra supplemental milk and milk without using techniques that do not involve breastfeeding.
- As there is an increase in skin-to-skin touch, the bonding between you and your baby will increase.
- Your baby will get to practice sucking on breasts and it will increase his grip on them.
- SNS is very supportive, not only of milk supply but also breastfeeding associations.
- SNS feeding will also enable you to get rid of frequent pumping to stimulate your breasts as your baby is acting as a natural stimulator.
- Helps mamas to get rid of nipple confusion and bottle preference in their babies.
- Continued stimulation of breasts increases the milk flow.
- The baby always gets his mouth full of milk which enhances his desire for breastfeeding.

DISADVANTAGES OF SNS FEEDING

Tube feeding is an easy process but it can be challenging for some mamas especially if it is introduced to a baby who is 3-4 weeks old. Older babies are capable of knowing the presence of a tube inside their mouth and they may reject it. But you should not give up as SNS can work perfectly with older babies as it was a success for me. For me, one successful tube feeding in a day was a big achievement when my baby became older.

It takes practice and it can go wrong which can be converted into frustration for mama. It can also demotivate some moms who are already in distress due to low milk supply. But continued trying can bring tube feeding to a successful outcome.

SNS has some disadvantages:

- **Difficult to use:** Until she masters using it, SNS can be a challenge for mama.
- **Difficult to clean:** Sometimes cleaning the tubes becomes messy work and it is impossible to clean them completely. You mostly have to replace them with new ones.
- **Doesn't fit every baby:** Some babies are not able to suck milk from the tube and others may get very low milk. Older babies may get to feel that there is something other than the nipple in their mouth and try to spit the tube out.
- **Can affect latching on:** If the baby becomes aware of the tube attached to the nipple, he'll not latch on properly or may refuse to breastfeed. Changing the breastfeeding position can help to get a proper latch-on.
- **Gagging:** If the tube gets deep into the baby's mouth it

may cause gagging or throwing up. Taping the tube onto the breast properly can help you avoid this.

- **Clog formation:** Reconstructed formula milk can form clogs and block the tube.

HOW LONG WILL YOU HAVE TO USE SNS?

The period of using SNS feeding depends on the reason you started using it in the first place. If you have a permanently low milk supply, you may have to adopt SNS feeding for the whole nursing period or until your baby is ready to take a bottle and handle it by himself.

It also can be for a few days or weeks if you only want your baby to get back to a normal breastfeeding routine and get rid of nipple refusal.

GIVEAWAY

A FREE GIFT FOR OUR READERS!

Five adaptable recipes you can download and start your breastfeeding journey off on a delicious foot!! Visit this link

KimberlyNicoleWhittaker.com

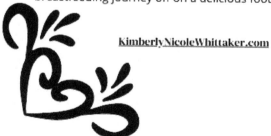

BOTTLE FEEDING

*a*lthough breastfeeding is the best choice for feeding the baby until he turns two years old, there are many circumstances and conditions when moms have to go with bottle feeding. Bottle feeding is a very different process to breastfeeding and you need to learn how to do it properly.

You should know the types of bottles and then select the best one for your baby. You can feed formula milk or your breastmilk (expressed) in a bottle to your baby. Your baby will also need to learn how to bottle feed and it may take a little time for the baby to get used to it and master it.

Most newborns have very little trouble in learning how to feed on a bottle nipple especially if the bottle is introduced in the early days. Sucking movements come naturally into babies. Bottle feeding can have many benefits besides making life a little easier for moms.

If your baby is used to bottle feeding, even your partner or a babysitter can feed him easily and you can get some much-needed rest from a tiring routine. For most working ladies, bottle feeding is the easiest tool for feeding a baby and maintaining a work balance.

The selection of the right formula is discussed in the next chapters. In this chapter, I'll show you how to master the art of bottle feeding.

WHEN TO INTRODUCE A BOTTLE

There is no proper time to introduce your baby to bottle feeding. Most lactation experts say that before starting with bottle feeding you should wait until breastfeeding is well settled and your breastmilk flow becomes steady.

The best time to introduce bottle feeding is probably between 3-4 weeks after childbirth. These weeks are very important to establish a breastfeeding routine and for your breasts to become completely stimulated to produce a regular flow of milk.

If you delay introducing a bottle to your baby for several weeks, he may strongly refuse to take it. If you cannot express breastmilk due to a medical issue or your milk is not enough to satisfy the baby's hunger, you should start bottle feeding from the very first day.

WHY SOME MAMAS CHOOSE BOTTLE-FEEDING

There can be many possible reasons for mamas to start bottle feeding. Sometimes it is just a normal part of feeding a baby when he needs formula milk. Sometimes it may have a specific reason behind it. Here are a few reasons why mamas start bottle-feeding their babies:

- The mama has a low supply of milk.
- The mama is experiencing nipple problems like sore nipples.
- Mama is not able to handle the baby and she wants someone else to feed him.
- The mama has to return to work and leave the baby with a babysitter.
- Mama feels it is hard to breastfeed in public.
- The baby is becoming weak and he needs some formula milk or supplements.
- The baby has grown and breastmilk is not enough to suffice his hunger.
- The mama has gone through a Cesarean section and she is not able to handle the baby.

CHOOSING THE RIGHT BOTTLES AND NIPPLES

When it comes to selecting bottles and nipples for your baby, you will see so many options and qualities. It can be hard to decide which bottle to pick for your baby. You can take advice from experienced mamas or can buy a few different types of bottles and give them a test try with your baby. You'll know which of them is best for your baby.

Every baby loves different types of bottles with different sizes and textures. It can become very difficult for you to select one from many options. Try a bottle for 5-7 days before declaring it a failure because some babies might take a few days to adjust to a bottle.

Mamas, let me tell you about some of the different types of bottles and nipples, and then you can select one for your baby.

Types of baby bottles

THERE ARE a lot of types and brands of bottles but they can be divided into these major types:

- **Standard bottles:** These classic-shaped bottles work best for a lot of babies. They are available in plastic, glass, and even stainless-steel.
- **Neck-angle bottles:** These bottles are designed in a way that they have a bend at the neck which prevents air from becoming stuck in. This makes feeding easier and prevents babies from getting gas problems. However, they may be hard to clean due to the angle.
- **Liner disposable bottles:** These bottles are made up of a very hard shell that holds the milk in a separate pouch. This bag-like pouch pinches as the baby finishes the feeding. This prevents air from getting in and reduces gassiness. As the bag-like pouches are disposable, they don't require cleaning and save a lot of time. They look like an easy option but they are not eco-friendly.
- **Wide-necked bottles:** Smart and thick, these bottles have a wide opening which in turn has a wider nipple than usual bottles. It enhances the bottle-feeding experience for both the mama and the baby. It is best for those babies who are going to transit between breastfeeding and bottle feeding regularly. As it is wider, it is easy to clean.

- **Vented bottles:** A built-in tube is present inside these bottles which don't allow the formation of air pockets in the bottle or nipple. They are harder to clean due to the vents and other extra parts.

Any of these bottles can work best for your baby. If not, there are many other types available on the market. Of course, every mama wants the best thing for her babies.

Types of nipples

NIPPLES USUALLY COME with bottles as a part of them but they can also be bought separately. They come in a diversity of shapes, dimensions, and types. This can help if your baby needs some special bottle feeding. Just like with bottles, try different types of nipples and choose the one that suits your baby best.

- **Standard nipples:** These are ball-shaped or elliptical and mostly come with the bottles. These are considered best for most babies.
- **Orthodontic nipples:** These nipples are best designed for the safety of the baby's palate. They have a bulging top and a flat base.
- **Flat-topped nipples:** These nipples very nicely mimic the shape of breast nipples. These contain a big bulb-like base and a flat top.
- **Anti-vacuum nipples:** These nipples have an anti-vacuum ability which is best suited to preventing gassiness and colic. It limits the amount of air the baby takes in while feeding.
- **Multi-flow nipples:** These nipples have a special design that allows different stages of the flow of milk in the same nipple. You can adjust the position of the nipple at

different stages like stage 1 or 2. These stages control the milk and make it slower or faster.

- **Disposable nipples:** These nipples come in different shapes but they are only for one-time use. They're easy to discard after every feeding session and there's, therefore, no worry about the cleaning process.

Always pick a bottle and nipple which your baby likes the most, is easy to clean, and has a simple design. The shape and feel of the nipple should also be considered before choosing it.

CHOOSING THE SIZE OF BOTTLES

Choosing the size of the bottles depends upon the age of your baby and the amount of milk he needs in one feed. Most newborns drink up to 3-4 ounces of milk in one feeding. So smaller bottles like 5 ounces bottles are best to begin with. The nipple of these bottles should have stage 1 milk flow (very little flow suitable for newborns in their first few weeks).

As babies keep on growing, they start to need more milk in a single feeding such as 8 ounces. They can also cope with a faster flow of milk from the nipple like stage 2 flow. So, mama should choose a bigger bottle now.

Babies more than 6 months old need stage 3 milk flow and bigger bottles as their tummies have grown bigger and need more milk to suffice their hunger.

HOW OFTEN THE BABY SHOULD BOTTLE FEED

If you want to continue bottle feeding along with breastfeeding, you should give the bottle to the baby 3-4 times a week. A maximum of once a day is enough. This is because too much bottle-feeding can lead to nipple confusion and the baby may refuse to breastfeed.

CLEANING THE BOTTLE-FEEDING SUPPLIES

Your infant's immune system is not very strong so you should keep everything related to the baby's feeding germ-free. For this purpose, you have to clean the bottle-feeding supplies after every use and clean them properly. This includes cleaning bottle nipples, rings, caps, bottles, spoons (if you are formula feeding), and valves. Wipe down the surface where you keep these supplies with bleach or disinfectant and wash your hands with soap and water before preparing feeds or handling the bottles. You should first wash the supplies with hot water, then rinse them in cold water. Steam or boil the supplies to sanitize them.

Replace the bottles and nipples approximately once a month. Clean the supplies after every feed and sanitize the supplies once a day. Discard the leftover milk in the bottle right away – don't let it remain in the bottle and never reuse it.

HOW TO BOTTLE FEED YOUR BABY

For some mamas, bottle feeding seems more like a technical process and there is a procedure to be followed.

Preparing the bottle

FIRST, you need to warm the bottle of milk. There are several ways to do this. The easiest is to put hot water into a jug and stand the bottle in this for a few minutes. Shake the milk to distribute the heat evenly. Alternatively, you can run the bottle under warm to hot water. Specialized bottle warmers are also available on the market which heat the milk to a specified temperature. Remember never to microwave a bottle of baby milk –it leaves hot spots on the bottle which cause problems.

If you are feeding pumped breastmilk to your baby, you don't need to warm it unless it is coming from the refrigerator or some other cold storage. Reheat stored breastmilk in the same way as described above. If you are giving formula in the bottle, you'll need to mix the proper amount of formula and warm water in the bottle (you'll learn everything about formula feeding in the next chapters).

Don't add any cereal to the bottle whether you are feeding pumped breastmilk or formula. Cereal should always be fed by spoon or feeding syringes.

Testing the bottle

BEFORE OFFERING the bottle to the baby, shake well to mix in any lumps (if formula milk) and shake gently (if breastmilk). Check the milk's temperature before giving it to the baby and make sure it is not hot. Putting a few drops of milk on your palm or inside of the wrist is the best way to check the temperature of the milk. Make sure milk is tepid, never hot. You can now give it to your baby.

Getting into position

SIT with your baby for a few minutes before starting bottle feeding and create a comfortable and relaxing environment. Hold the baby in such a way that his head and neck are well supported with your arm or hand. Make sure your baby is not laying completely flat – he should be upright at a 45-degree angle with proper alignment of his head and neck. Place a pillow or some support under your arm so it doesn't get fatigued.

Don't tip the bottle fully up or completely down but keep it at a slight angle. This allows for the milk to flow out at the right speed – neither too fast nor too slow. It also prevents the baby from swallowing too much air which would give him gas problems.

Don't keep the baby on the same side until he finishes the bottle, but change his side or position of feeding. This mimics changing sides for breastfeeding, gives him something new to look at, and keeps you both comfortable while feeding.

Checking the nipple

DON'T GET DISTRACTED as your baby starts feeding with the bottle but keep an eye on his face and listen out for the sounds he makes while sipping the milk. If the baby makes a loud sound of gulping and sputtering and if the milk is dripping out from the sides of his mouth, then the milk flow is probably too fast. Make sure to tilt the bottle downwards to slow the flow down.

On the other hand, if the baby is getting frustrated or sucking hard, the flow of milk from the bottle may be too slow. You can tilt the bottle upward or can loosen the tight grip of the cap of the bottle. This will increase the flow of milk into the nipple. If it doesn't work, try changing the nipple for one with a bigger hole.

Finishing the feeding

YOU HAVE to keep an eye out for signs that the baby is full. He will push the nipple out of his mouth with his tongue and will not accept it on trying again or he will fall asleep.

Once you know that the baby has finished the feeding, take the bottle away, hold him upright and rub his back until he burps. Most babies fall asleep right after finishing a feeding. Once you've put him down for a nap, take the bottle away and discard any remaining milk. Never keep it for later. Wash the bottle with hot water and soap and disinfect it.

Clean the nipple also with warm water and let the bottle remain open and upside-down for a while to dry.

TIPS FOR BOTTLE-FEEDING

- Bottle-feed the baby when the atmosphere is relaxing and calm. Try playing with the baby before giving him the bottle to turn his mood into happiness and joy. This will encourage him to take the bottle and will make it easy for mama. However, if he's really hungry and crying for food, the best thing to do is feed him asap!
- Let the baby play with the bottle and enjoy it. It doesn't matter if he takes it out from his mouth for a while, keep on giving him the bottle as long as he is enjoying it.

- Do not forget to warm the bottle and nipples before feeding.
- If it is doable for you, you are recommended to use freshly pumped breastmilk instead of a frozen one. Some of the anti-infective properties are lost when freezing.
- If you have no other choice but to use frozen breastmilk, make sure to warm it up and shake it gently before giving it to the baby.
- In the start, give your baby a nipple that has a slow flow of milk. Once bottle feeding is established, you can switch to a faster-flow nipple.
- Hey, Mama! Always try to keep a positive attitude towards bottle feeding and do not make it difficult for yourself.

PACED FEEDING

*T*here's no doubt that breastfeeding is the most important thing for your baby. It is hands-down the best way to feed your little one. However, sometimes it becomes a challenge to continue properly and you need help by bottle-feeding your baby. However, if bottle feeding is not properly done, nipple confusion can happen and it will cause difficulties in breastfeeding.

Here is a bottle-feeding technique called "paced feeding" that is said to exactly mimic breastfeeding.

Yes, this is true! Paced feeding is a slower, steadier bottle-feeding method.

Paced feeding is a bottle-feeding process in which you slow down the milk supply to the nipples and your baby feeds at his own pace, whether slow or fast. It allows the baby to fully control his feeding sessions and the amount of milk he wants. It is just like natural breastfeeding – slow, precise, and infant-controlled.

If you are bottle-feeding your baby with or without breastfeeding, you need to know about paced feeding. Paced feeding is becoming very common among new mamas because it is one of the best bottle-feeding techniques which helps your infants to feed at their own pace.

However you are feeding your baby – either with breast or formula – you will probably need to bottle feed him at some point. However, you need to be careful about starting bottle feeding because it can be very difficult to make your baby feed with a bottle.

Your baby may not accept bottle feeding at all or he can get used to it and may get nipple confusion and refuse to breastfeed. So, this is why I recommend paced feeding which is very similar to breastfeeding. There are very low chances of breast confusion or rejection when using paced bottle feeding.

Paced feeding also minimizes the risk of overfeeding which may cause distress to the baby. This feeding technique is suggested for all babies who either completely rely on bottle-feeding or get bottle-fed along with breastfeeding.

PACED FEEDING IS A LIFESAVING HACK

There come so many situations in a mama's life when she may need to bottle feed her baby. Maybe due to her job routines or her other life engagements. In such difficult scenarios, paced bottle-feeding becomes an essential and lifesaving tool for a mama. It can help you in the following situations:

- When you are about to transfer your baby to bottle feeding from breastfeeding and your baby doesn't like to bottle feed. Paced feeding will give him a sense of breastfeeding so that he can get used to it.
- When you want a balance between bottle feeding and breastfeeding and you don't want to suffer from nipple confusion or your baby to start favoring bottle-feeding over your breasts.
- If you have to go to work and leave your baby with a babysitter, paced feeding is most important. If the babysitter will use paced feeding either with your pumped breastmilk or formula milk, you will not lose out on bonding with your baby. It will also prevent your baby from being overfed.
- When your baby is having stomach issues like gas or colic while bottle feeding, paced feeding will help them feed on lower and more normal quantities of milk which will not be a burden on their upset stomach.
- If your baby is getting overwhelmed by the fast flow of a bottle, he may reject bottle feeding. Paced feeding can come in at this time and it will make your baby more comfortable.

HOW TO DO PACED FEEDING

There is no exact technique for paced feeding but I can give you some principles. You will have to come up with the most comfortable way for you and your baby. Here are the main things to remember:

- Keep it slow. Let your baby take pauses and breathe.
- Do not overfeed your baby. When they show signs of fullness, stop feeding.
- Stay connected to them and help them feel closeness.

PACED FEEDING STEPS

Paced feeding may be different with every mom and child, but some important aspects can be followed to make it a perfect fit.

Baby position

YOUR BABY SHOULD ALWAYS BE HELD in an upright position. If not held upright, he shall be sloped back only slightly. Your baby should be resting in your lap. For very young babies, you should support their head and neck with your other hand and arm to help them stay upright.

Always give them eye contact. This will give them a feeling of comfort and relaxation.

Offering the bottle

TICKLE the baby's upper lip with your finger or, most commonly, with the tip of the nipple. This will trigger the baby to open his mouth and try to latch onto the bottle for feeding.

Make your baby open his mouth more widely so that the nipple of the bottle fits into his mouth and he can suck properly.

The most important thing while paced feeding is that you should keep the bottle horizontal instead of vertical. This will slow down the milk flow which is what makes this feeding process steady and comfortable. Make sure the bottle's nipple is not full all the time. It should be half-filled which will prevent overflow of milk into the baby's mouth.

Paced feeding will let your baby learn to control his feedings and have a proper sense of when he will be full. With this method, the baby is not filling his belly before the signals of fullness travel to his response center in the brain.

You should also contemplate stopping the milk from going into the nipple for a few seconds by tilting the bottle flatter. This will completely mimic the letdown behavior of breastfeeding which comes naturally and will reduce the chances of breast preference.

Pausing

TAKE the nipple out of the baby's mouth by tipping down the bottle slowly after regular intervals of 40-60 seconds and give your baby a break as happens naturally in breastfeeding. If your baby is taking pauses on his own, that is a good thing.

You can also pause feeding by leaning the baby towards the bottle and stopping the flow of milk to the baby's mouth.

Switch sides

KEEP SWITCHING the sides the baby is on from one arm to the other to mimic side switching in breastfeeding. Keep watching your baby and giving him smiles all the time. This will allow the baby to feel more connected and affectionate.

Ending the feeding

USUALLY, overfeeding becomes an issue while bottle feeding. This is why you should keep an eye on the signs which tell you that the baby is full and now is the time to stop feeding. Usually, babies give the following signs when they are full:

- Slow down their sucking speed
- Their eyes start wandering
- They fall asleep
- They open their hands and relax them

When you think your baby is becoming full, stop feeding by taking away the bottle gently. Offer it again by tickling their lips. If they accept it again, allow them to have 10-12 more sucks. Repeat taking the bottle away and offering it again until they refuse to take it back. This is the best way to know the proper fullness of your baby.

Similarly, don't make the baby finish the complete bottle if he is full with less milk. Once the baby shows that he's full, take away the bottle and let him relax or sleep.

Try paced feeding

As a MAMA of three children who is currently feeding my third one, I know you've probably been told so many rules and regulations about doing things for your babies. Just keep in mind that although paced feeding has proper procedures and a set of rules, you should go with what makes you comfortable with your baby. Rules are not set in stone but should be treated as guidelines. Just take what is working for you and your baby and leave the rest.

Meanwhile, if you are having trouble with bottle feeding your baby or trying to transition him between breastfeeding and bottle feeding, do try paced bottle feeding. You just have to practice and you will soon master it.

We mamas only have one goal – we want what is best and healthiest for our babies and most of us will do anything to achieve that. Paced bottle feeding is the best technique to achieve this goal. The main thing to remember is that it doesn't matter how you do it, feeding your baby should be about nourishment, bonding, and love.

NIPPLE CONFUSION

Nipple confusion can happen when you start bottle feeding or you give a dummy nipple to your baby to suck. Your baby may become confused about the bottle's nipple and the breast and he may reject your nipple while breastfeeding. Don't worry, it is merely confusion and it can be corrected with a very simple method which we'll discuss later in this chapter.

When your baby starts sucking a bottle nipple or dummy teat, he needs to suck differently than the natural sucking mechanism needed to breastfeed. This can change your baby's perception about sucking and in the early days or weeks can cause nipple confusion.

Bottle nipples or dummy teats have comparatively rigid nipples that require more force for sucking than breastfeeding. Similarly, bottle feeding provides the baby with a constant flow of milk and he doesn't need to struggle with milk letdowns that happen in breastfeeding. This makes it easy for the baby to fill his tummy with a constant supply of milk, and when he breastfeeds, he may refuse it because it will require him to work harder to get full.

There are many mechanical and sucking differences between breastfeeding and bottle feeding. The baby tries to use the bottle-feeding technique while breastfeeding and fails to latch on and suck. Nipple confusion can even lead to breast refusal.

HOW BABIES SUCK ON THE BREAST

To get milk from the breasts, the baby needs to coordinate tongue and jaw movements to create a sucking motion that is exclusive to breastfeeding. To latch on properly, the baby needs to open his mouth wide and get the stretchable nipple into his mouth and also get a proper lip grip on the areola. Baby's gums compress the milk sacs present under the areola and the tongue milks the breast with a wave-like motion from front to back. This brings the milk down from the areola to the nipple and finally into the baby's mouth.

HOW BABIES SUCK ON A BOTTLE

Sucking from a bottle is completely different than breastfeeding. Due to the downward tilting of the bottle, gravity plays a role in the downflow of milk into the baby's mouth and he doesn't have to suck with much force. Also, the baby doesn't have to open his mouth as wide as in breastfeeding to form a tight grip. The bottle nipple is not taken deeply into the mouth and the sucking movement of the tongue is also not needed. Baby can just slightly move his lips and gums to get milk into his mouth. Milk flow is constant from the bottle, there is no letdown like in breastfeeding, and the baby can get full in a shorter time.

THE CONFUSION

Nipple confusion happens when the baby tries to apply the bottle feeding technique to the breast. We can easily see the difference by looking into illustrations of an artificial nipple with that of breastfeeding.

If the baby sucked your nipples just as he sucked the nipple of the bottle, it would hurt you and cause sore nipples. Babies try to use up and down movement of their tongues on breasts just like they do in bottle feeding and they may push your nipple out of their mouth. Babies don't completely open their mouths and they become unable to feed on breasts.

Also, babies become used to the constant flow of milk from the bottle and they want the same from their mama's breasts. Babies have to suck for one to two minutes to stimulate the natural flow of milk from breasts while in the bottle it starts flowing just after they take a nipple in their mouth.

These things cause nipple confusion.

SIGNS OF NIPPLE CONFUSION

These are some common signs which tell you about nipple confusion:

- Baby pushes her tongue upwards while sucking which pushes your nipple out of her mouth.
- He doesn't open his mouth wide enough to fit your nipple and areola in his mouth.
- She shows frustration that mama's milk isn't coming out immediately after taking a nipple in her mouth just like bottle feeding.

PREVENTING NIPPLE CONFUSION

It is easier to prevent nipple confusion than undo it (which is, however, possible). Nipple confusion can be prevented by following and keeping in mind some facts listed below:

- Don't rush into starting giving the bottle to your baby in the first few weeks after birth. First, try to establish proper breastfeeding until it feels like an everyday routine.
- Establish a comfortable routine and position for you and your baby to be relaxed when feeding.
- If your baby is disliking the delay of milk coming out of your breasts, help yourself with pumping so the baby can get milk right away when he starts sucking.
- Don't wait until your baby is very hungry before starting to feed him. Make a timetable and try to establish a feeding schedule.

HOW TO UNDO NIPPLE CONFUSION

Nipple confusion is not a big problem and it can be undone with just a few simple precautions and methods:

- **Decrease the use of bottles and pacifiers** – Although your baby may need them at some stage, you can minimize nipple confusion by using these less and rather trying to develop a breastfeeding routine.
- **Decrease the use of artificial nipples** – If your baby needs some supplemental feeding, use droppers or a spoon to feed him instead of using nipples and bottles.
- **Re-establish the charm of breastfeeding** – Give your baby more skin-to-skin contact near your breasts and try to please him by carrying him near your breasts.

- **Create calmness before breastfeeding** – Try to make the baby feel calm and relaxed before trying to breastfeed or find a time when your baby is calm and happy.
- **Work on the proper latch-on technique** – Try new positions for latching-on and make your baby feel comfortable in the best way he likes. Wait until he opens his mouth completely wide before putting a nipple into it.
- **Try to teach the baby** – Open your mouth and say, "open" while looking at your baby. Sometimes infants try to mimic the actions of adults, especially that of their moms.
- **Try to pump your breasts** – Try pumping your breasts before breastfeeding. It will provide your baby with milk instantly after he's latched on. It will save your baby from pre-sucking the breast to stimulate it for milk flow.
- **Give your baby a starter** – Try putting a few drops of your pumped breastmilk into his mouth with a dropper or feeding syringe. This will give your baby a prior taste of your milk and he will then latch on properly.

Give your baby proper time to learn his way back to breastfeeding by tiny steps. It may take a few days for the baby to come back to the breasts properly.

FORMULA FEEDING

WHAT IS FORMULA FEEDING?

*F*ormula milk or feeding is a specially manufactured breastmilk substitute for babies that can be used along with breastmilk, or as an alternative to it.

It is used by mamas who can't breastfeed or do not want to continue breastfeeding anymore. It's also used by mamas who are busy in their daily routine. Whatever the reason is, mama should not feel guilty about her decision.

The thought of not breastfeeding a child can be very troublesome for some mamas as they believe they are not bonding properly with their child. But the mama needs to accept that a loving mama makes a very special bond with her baby irrespective of the way she feeds him. All your baby needs is to stay happy and healthy, so don't stress about using formula milk.

Apart from breastmilk, formula milk is the only product that the medical community approves as nutritionally acceptable for babies who are under the age of one year. Goats and cows' milk is not recommended for small babies.

IS FORMULA MILK SAFE?

When a mama has to feed formula milk to her baby, the first thing that may come to her mind is, **"Is formula milk safe?"** because breastmilk offers irreplaceable nutrition.

Formula milk gives all the nutrients that are needed for a baby's growth and development. However, formula milk does not have the same health benefits for your baby and you as well, as compared to breastmilk. It does not protect your child from infections.

Your health advisor can guide you with all the information that you need to know about whether the formula is safe or if your baby can be fed with it.

WHAT'S IN FORMULA MILK?

Ingredients differ from country to country and from product to product, but formula milk is mostly made of refined skimmed cow's milk with the addition of emulsifiers and stabilizers that benefit the mixing of oil and water when you make the feed. The formula milk may also contain:

- Lactose
- Enzymes and amino acids
- Vitamins and minerals extracted from plant and animal sources
- Probiotics (in some formulas)
- Fatty acids
- Plant-based oils

DIFFERENT TYPES OF FORMULAS

If you have decided to feed formula milk to your baby then you also need to decide which kind of milk will be best for your baby's health. You need to know about the different types of formula milk and their benefits.

There are a lot of nutritionally sound formula choices that are said to replicate nature's good direction. Whereas no formula contains the immune molecules passed to the baby through mama's milk, several have identical varieties and portions of carbohydrates, fats, proteins, minerals, and vitamins.

Some typical types of baby formula feedings are:

- Milk-based, iron-fortified formula

Babies younger than a year old cannot digest unprocessed cows' milk properly. It's tough to digest and does not offer the entire nutritional spectrum that developing babies need. However, most of the formula feedings use cow's milk reformed for human babies.

The proteins are made easy to digest, lactose is added to a lot of closely parallel breastmilk and vegetable oil is substituted for the animal fat.

Iron is important for a baby's growth and development so most pediatricians suggest an iron-fortified formula for many babies at least till their first birthday.

- Hydrolyzed formula

The protein content in this kind of formula is in smaller protein molecules that make it easy for babies to digest. That's the reason it is also called a digestible *formula*. It is usually lactose-free too. It is usually recommended for allergy-prone babies.

There are plenty of thoughts about shifting to hydrolyzed or maybe partly hydrolyzed formula. For one, it is usually costly, therefore, make sure to speak to your specialist about choices for bottle-feeding an allergic-prone child before you use that alternative.

- Soy-based formula

Soy-based formulas are made from soybeans with added minerals, vitamins, and other nutrients.

As a result, soy formulas differ more from human milk than cow milk. They are not usually recommended as an alternative drink except under certain circumstances, for example, if your baby is allergic to cow's milk. It's common for infants with a milk allergy to also be sensitive to soy protein.

- Special formula

SOME BOTTLE-FED INFANTS need special formulas. These include premature infants, babies that are allergic to both soy formula and cow's milk, and babies with metabolic disorders.

These special baby formula products are not recommended or necessary unless your specialist says so. They are lactose-free, hypoallergenic, and particularly easy to digest.

- Organic formula

These come from milk products that are created without the utilization of herbicides, pesticides, antibiotics, and growth hormones. For that reason, they are considered healthier by some doctors.

Some organic child formulas contain cane sugar, which is considerably sweeter than the sugars most commonly used in formulas. Some consultants worry that they may contribute to some health issues like excess weight gain and cavities. However, not all organic formulas use sucrose. If you still have queries, ask your pediatrician.

- Probiotic and prebiotic formula

Some formulas for infants are fortified with probiotics or microorganisms (bacteria) that are said to stop diarrhea in otherwise healthy children.

Probiotics must not be given to chronic or seriously ill infants, and also the jury is still out on whether or not they help to treat diarrhea or stop the other conditions.

Prebiotics are also put into some formulas to decrease infections in healthy babies, however, it's still unknown whether or not they are effective.

HOW MUCH FORMULA MILK SHOULD A BABY TAKE?

Newly born babies start with a very small amount of formula. The amount is calculated according to their energy needs and weight. Here is a guide:

- **In the first few days:** Newborn formula-feeding babies can take 2 to 3 ounces (60 to 90 ml) of formula per feeding every three to four hours on average throughout their initial few weeks.
- **During the first few weeks:** If your baby is sleeping

longer than 4 to 5 hours and starts omitting feedings, then wake them up and provide them a bottle feed.

- **At the end of the first month:** Your baby will take at least 4 ounces (120 ml) per feeding every 4 hours.
- **Two-month-old baby:** Your baby will consume at least 3-6 ounces (90-180 ml) every three to four hours. That adds up to about 18-32 ounces (540-960 ml) in a day.
- **Three-month-old baby:** The baby will take 4-6 ounces (120-180 ml) of formula about every four hours. This adds up to about 24-36 ounces (720-1080 ml) of formula in about six feedings a day.
- **Four-month-old baby:** The baby will drink 5-7 ounces (150-210 ml) of formula every four to five hours. It increases to 24 to 32 ounces (720-960 ml) of formula in an entire feeding of four to six feedings a day.
- **Five-month-old baby:** Your baby will often take 6 to 8 ounces (180-240 ml) of formula about five times a day. This adds up to 24 to 36 ounces (720-1080 ml) of formula in 24 hours.
- **Six-month-old baby:** Your baby will take 6 to 8 ounces (180-240 ml) of formula in four or five feedings every 24 hours. This adds up to 24 to 32 ounces (720-960 ml) of formula in a whole day.

USE OF FORMULA FEEDING

The use of formula feed is common. Here are some of the most usual reasons for not breastfeeding a child:

- Mama's health

Doctors recommend formula feeding if the mama has some serious infection or disease which can be transferred to a baby by her milk. As we have discussed earlier, if mama has active tuberculosis, HIV, breast cancer, or any fatal disease, she is advised not to breastfeed her child.

- Absence of mama

A mama and her baby may become separated for many reasons. The child may be adopted or an orphan. The mother may be in hospital for some treatment purpose In such situations, the child is fed formula milk.

- The baby is unable to breastfeed

The baby may have a birth defect or error of metabolism such as galactosemia. Galactosemia makes the body unable to convert galactose (a sugar found in breastmilk) to glucose. Due to this, the baby may face difficulty in breastfeeding.

- Food allergies

The food consumed by a mama may arouse an allergic reaction in the baby. In this situation, the mama has to pay attention to which food her baby is reacting to and stop taking that food. However, if the baby is still allergic to her milk then she needs to ask a doctor who may advise feeding formula milk to prevent the baby from getting allergic reactions.

- Lactation insufficiency

The mama is not able to produce enough milk for her baby. She will then use formula milk as a breastmilk supplement.

HOW TO CHOOSE THE RIGHT FORMULA

You have made up your mind to formula feed your baby but choosing the right formula for a baby can be stressful to parents. There are many options on the market, making choosing one confusing. The main point is that you need to know about the needs of your baby before selecting the formula. The formula you select must be able to fulfill the baby's needs and help him in his growth and development.

SOME IMPORTANT THINGS WHILE BUYING A FORMULA

- Ingredients of the formula and its similarity to breastmilk
- Production quality and organic formula
- Availability and sourcing
- Cost of the formula

These are the main priorities that many parents consider. Let's discuss them in detail.

- Ingredients of formula and its similarity to breastmilk

Even though no formula is capable of replacing the way breastmilk boosts the immune system, the ingredients of most formula milk are created to approach the nutrition of nursing as far as possible.

Such kinds of formulas are a mixture of fats, proteins, vitamins, carbohydrates, minerals, and micronutrients that are found in breastmilk. They also use the same source for carbohydrates (lactose). These formulas are known as European formulas.

These formulas also offer stages that recreate breastmilk's changing composition over time.

If you want a formula that is closely related to breastmilk then one with a European formula is the one for you.

- Production quality and organic formula

Organic products are ones whose ingredients are produced without regular application of pesticides or fertilizers and are produced without artificial nutrients (man-made ingredients). Organic products do not hold any type of chemical pesticides.

Choosing the best formula milk that fulfills the needs of your baby is a difficult and important decision for parents. The first year of a baby's life is a time of rapid growth. Choosing the right formula helps set them on the road to healthy growth and development.

If the parents choose an organic formula, it gives them peace of mind that they are giving their baby effective, pure milk that's free from hormones and antibiotics, has minimal chemical residues, and contains no genetically changed ingredients.

- Availability and sourcing

Some parents value the convenience of being able to go into their local store to purchase the formula as soon as they need it. Other parents find it more convenient to have formula delivered to their house directly by shopping online. Many parents preferred online shopping during the COVID-19 pandemic because it was hard to purchase anything in the local stores. The source from where you are purchasing is very important. Purchase formulas from a trusted retailer from where you are sure about the freshness, quality, and availability of the product.

- Cost of formula

Formula feeding is expensive! Before choosing a formula, many parents consider the price of the formula according to their budget.

HOW WOULD YOU KNOW IF YOUR BABY HAS AN ALLERGY?

Milk allergies in babies are uncommon and only affect 3 to 4 percent of babies. Many mamas don't know how to tell the difference between their baby having a milk allergy or being intolerant to milk or lactose.

For babies that have an allergic reaction to milk, the baby's immune system reacts negatively to the proteins in the cow's milk. The allergic baby feeding on breastmilk reacts to the dairy that his mama has consumed. Allergic formula-feeding babies react to the cow's milk protein within the formula.

On the other hand, milk intolerance has no concern with the cow's milk protein or immune system but it has to do with the digestive system. If milk intolerant, your baby may have loose stools or blood in his stool.

How would a mama diagnose if her baby is allergic to milk? Here are some symptoms of milk allergy in babies:

- Vomiting
- Constantly spitting up
- Abdominal pain
- Diarrhea
- Hives
- Blood in stool
- Skin rashes

- Swelling (of mouth and throat)
- Coughing
- Watery eyes
- Stuffy nose

And some symptoms of lactose intolerance of babies are:

- Bloated stomach
- Gas
- Failure to gain weight
- Spitting up
- Irritability or crying

If you suspect that your baby is milk intolerant or allergic, please do not try to diagnose it yourself. Before changing his feeding, have him checked by your doctor or pediatrician.

IS IT IMPORTANT TO CHOOSE A FORMULA FOR THE RIGHT AGE GROUP?

The best way to use formulas is to read the instructions on the can. The instructions will tell you how to mix it, how much to feed the baby at different ages and weights, and what ages the formula is appropriate for. If you are still confused, your health advisor can guide you properly.

Formulas labeled "Starter", "Newborn", and "Step 1" are specially designed for babies from birth till year 1.

"Step 2", "Progress", and "Follow on" formulas are used from the ages of 6 months to 1 year. Babies over 6 months in age have diverse nutritional needs so these formulas contain more iron and protein, and different amounts of minerals and vitamins that are quite different compared to the early infant formulas.

So, it's important to choose the correct age level formula for your baby because the nutritional needs of each age group are not the same.

IS THERE A DIFFERENCE BETWEEN BRANDS?

There is not an enormous difference between brands regarding fats, proteins, energy, carbohydrates, minerals, and vitamins. Parents will choose different ones depending on price and availability.

If you are thinking of switching from one brand to another, make sure to check the number of spoons required, and if the spoon number to the ratio of water is different.

It is strongly recommended not to change formula brands all the time. The taste of other brands is a little bit different and it may disturb the feeding routine of your baby. If you are considering changing the brand, do it under the guidance of your health professional.

IS ORGANIC BABY FORMULA BEST?

Formulas that are labeled "organic", can be trusted that the ingredients of that formula are not managed by using herbicides, pesticides, or any other harmful chemical during their production. If you prefer eating organic foods then you will probably want to use an organic formula for your baby as well.

The disadvantage of organic formulas is that they are up to 30 percent costlier than non-organic brands. If you can afford to buy organic formula, then by all means, use it but if it is not within your budget then don't worry too much because the non-organic formula brands are also tested and maintain high-quality standards to ensure their consumption is not harmful to babies.

BENEFITS OF SOY-BASED FORMULAS

Soy-based formulas are preferred by parents who adhere to a vegetarian or vegan diet. Soy formula is also an alternative to cow's milk formula if the symptoms of dairy allergy have been seen in your baby or he has tested positive for a dairy allergy. However, some babies that are allergic to cow's milk also have an intolerance to soy proteins. For such babies, a hydrolyzed formula could be a better option.

If we compare soy formula nutrients with those of other formulas, a soy-based formula has the same important nutrients and calories as other kinds of baby formulas. Hence, this formula has the same ability to fulfill the baby's need for growth and development.

However, some health organizations do not suggest its extensive use because they consider that it may offer a lesser nutritional advantage than cow's milk formula. Soy formula is usually suggested for vegetarian families.

WHAT ABOUT TRYING A BUNCH OF FORMULAS?

It is not usually suggested to check out different formulas. Because the production of formulas is heavily monitored, there is little difference between each brand. It would be a costly exercise to experiment with multiple baby formulas. More importantly, trying a bunch of formulas can cause disturbance in the baby's stomach. His feeding routine may become upset because the taste of brands is different. By trying different formulas, you may cause the baby to get constipation, painful gas, reflux, or explosive diarrhea.

Select the formula that you want to feed your baby, and stick to that only one unless your baby has problems with it. Do not change just because another brand is on sale that week.

CHOOSING THE RIGHT FORMULA FOR YOUR BABY

We have discussed many ideas that may help you with the selection of formula milk for your baby. Being a parent, there are many things to consider while taking any kind of step for your baby because it's all about his health.

The most important thing in the selection of formula milk is the age of your baby and whether he has any special nutritional needs. Closely follow your doctor's or other healthcare specialist's recommendations.

Here are some stages according to age for formula milk that is very important for parents to know:

- Newborn babies are called "1st stage" or "Stage 1".
- Six months to 12 months age is also known as "2nd stage", "Stage 2", or "Progress".
- The age from 1st birthday to 3 years is also known as "3rd stage", "Stage 3", or "Toddler".

Here are some additional tips that will help you to obtain the right formula for your baby:

- Talk to your pediatrician. He could suggest some unique latest formulas. He might have some samples available.
- If you don't have any suggestions or warnings from your pediatrician, use cow's milk formula first. There is no need to try specialized formulas such as soy-based formulas.
- Special formulas are used with the guidance of a

healthcare professional to make sure that they are suitable for your baby and so that they can observe your baby's growth and progress.

- Double-check that the formula you selected is fortified with vitamin D and iron as both of these are essential in a baby's growth. Some formulas are also enriched with DHA (an omega-3 fatty acid) that helps in the development of a baby's brain.
- Keep checking for any indications of discomfort with your baby such as crying, excessive spitting up, and restlessness.
- Contact your pediatrician or other mamas who are formula feeding their babies in case you have any questions regarding formula feeding. This will help you out with formula milk selection if you take feedback from the community of formula feeders.

PROCEDURES OF FORMULA FEEDING

Once you have selected a formula milk for your baby, the first step you have to do is to check the expiry date. If the can has expired or is somehow damaged, do not buy that one. When you buy the formula and you are going to prepare it, follow the given steps to prepare a bottle for the baby.

- **Wash your hands:** Before preparing a bottle for your baby, wash your hands with soap and warm water properly. You must prepare baby bottles with clean hands.
- **Prepare your bottle:** Purify the bottle, nipple, caps, and rings even when you are using them for the first time. If the water in your home is chlorinated, then you can purify the bottle and accessories with a dishwasher and then rinse them with hot water. If you are using non-

chlorinated water or well water, you can purify accessories by boiling them in water for five to ten minutes, or you can use a terminal heating process. In terminal heating, you cannot sterilize but you can clean the bottles in advance.

After using them for the first time, there is mostly no need to purify your accessories and bottles. You can simply wash them with soap or dishwasher with hot water. You can also clean the bottles with the help of brushes.

- **Add water to powdered formulas or liquid concentrate:** If you are using any of the formulas, whether powdered or liquid, you will need to add water to it. You can use any kind of water but it must be clean. If you are using tap water, boil it for one minute and let it cool to body temperature.
- **Measure the formula:** Measure the amount of formula and water carefully. If you add too much water it will not fill your baby's nutritional needs. If you add too little water, it may cause dehydration and diarrhea. Never try to make the formula mix "stronger" or "weaker".
- **Warm the formula if needed:** If you are using room temperature or even cold formula it's all fine. If your baby prefers warm formula then let the bottle sit in a jug of warm water for a few minutes or hold the bottle under hot running water. Before giving the warm formula to your baby, test to make sure it's not too hot by putting a few drops of milk onto the back of your hand or inside of your wrist. The milk should be lukewarm. Do not microwave it, because the milk will get too hot in patches and it will burn your baby's mouth.

- **Place your baby in a feeding position:** Hold the baby in a semi-upright position and support his/her head. Do not feed them lying down, because in this way milk can flow into their middle ear and can cause infection. To stop your baby from swallowing air when he/she sucks, lower the bottle in such a way that the formula milk covers the neck of the bottle and fills the nipple completely.

- **Burp your baby after feeding:** When babies swallow air throughout feeding, they get fussy and cranky. This happens a lot usually with bottle-fed babies but breastfeeding babies may also swallow air. To stop a tummy getting too much air, after every 2 to 3 ounces of feeding, burp your baby by sitting him upright. If your baby doesn't burp after a few minutes of attempting, carry on with feeding. The following are some good burping positions:

Over the shoulder: Put the baby over your shoulder and rub or pat his back.

On the lap: Place the baby upright on your lap, tilt his/her weight opposite to your hand, supporting his chest with one hand and patting his back with the other.

Lying down: Lie down your baby's stomach-down on your lap and rub or pat his back.

- **Toss leftovers:** After feeding your baby as much as he needs, throw away the milk that is left in the bottle because it may nurture bacteria even after refrigerating it. Never keep the leftovers as they may be harmful to your baby.

BOOB TO FOOD TRANSITION

*P*ediatricians suggest exclusive breastfeeding for the baby's first six months as well as a breastfeeding supplement until the baby turns one year old. (Formula milk is a good option for mamas who don't want to breastfeed.) Introducing babies to solid foods is a big step involving getting them used to chewing and swallowing food. However, it becomes essential after a year old to provide important nutritional benefits.

Some pediatricians say that parents should start their child on solids between four and six months, but the timing depends on your child. Introducing solid foods is very important for babies because it helps them to learn how to eat from a range of foods. They begin to experience new textures and tastes. Introducing solid foods to a baby before four months old is not recommended. Every child is different so how can parents know when their babies are ready for solid foods other than formula milk or breastmilk?

Here are some signs that show your baby is now ready to begin solid foods:

- They can hold up their heads and sit upright
- They will show an interest in foods when you are eating and stare at your plate
- They open their mouths when they are offered food or a spoon
- They still seem hungry after getting a full portion of breastmilk or formula milk in a day (about 8 to 10 breastfeeding sessions and 32 ounces of formula milk).

When you are introducing solid food to your baby for the first time, it's good to offer food when the baby is relaxed and happy. Give it in the morning in case there is a reaction. This will be more difficult to deal with at night.

Your babies will love to try solid foods after being fed formula or breastmilk because they still have space in their stomachs for new foods.

THE TEXTURE OF FOOD WHEN INTRODUCING SOLIDS

When your little one is ready for solid foods, his first food must be finely mashed or pureed to make it super-smooth smooth in texture. Later you will progress to a coarser mash and then soft pieces. Some babies will quickly move to minced foods while others gag at the slightest lump.

In adjusting to new textures, babies take some time. The child may gag, cough, or spit-up. As your baby's oral skills develop, lumpier and thicker food can be introduced. This process takes several months.

Some food could cause choking, thus it is important to feed your babies with foods that are the correct textures. To prevent choking, prepare foods that do not need chewing. Feed small portions of just a half teaspoon at a time, to begin with. Always keep an eye on your baby whenever he/she is eating.

Offering your baby many different food textures and flavors will assist your baby to learn how to chew the food and chewing in turn assists with speech development. It additionally encourages self-feeding and prevents feeding difficulties as your baby grows and develops.

WHAT CHANGES CAN BE EXPECTED IN BABIES AFTER SOLID FOODS?

After eating solid foods, babies' stools may vary in color and become more solid. Because of additional fats and sugars, the stools will have a much stronger smell too. Due to peas and other different green vegetables, the stool may become green in color, and beets might turn them a red color (Beets usually make urine a red color too). If the meal has not been strained, the baby's stool might contain undigested parts of food particularly corn, peas, tomato skins, and other vegetables. All of this is normal. The digestive system of the baby is still not completely developed and needs time before completely processing these new meals. If the stools are very loose, full of mucus, and watery it means that the digestive system is disturbed. In such a case, decrease the number of solids and try to present each new food more slowly. If the situation is still not in control and the baby's stool is still watery, talk to your doctor to find out the reason behind it.

HOW TO INTRODUCE SOLID FOODS AND HOW TO FEED THEM

When introducing solid foods, try to give single-ingredient meals to your child in the beginning. This will assist you in noticing if your child has any issues with the food, such as allergies. Wait for up to 5 days between every new food. Before you know it, your baby will be on his/her way to eating and enjoying several foods.

As soon as your child understands the idea of consumption and shows interest in mealtime (it typically happens between six to nine months), set their routine for breakfast, lunch, and dinner. Even though they may not be hungry sometimes, this will get them used to the concept of consumption on a schedule. Never pressurize your baby to eat food if they are not interested but simply take them out of their feeding chair and try again later.

When you are ready to feed your baby with solid foods, always start with half a spoon or less than that. During this feeding time try to keep talking with your baby saying things like, "Wow, look. This is so good!" In the beginning, babies do not know what to do. The baby might look confused, or may accept or reject the food depending on their mood. When the baby is relaxed, happy, and shows his interest in food it is the best time for giving them food.

To make feeding solid foods easier in the start, it is suggested first giving the baby a milk feed then moving to the solid food. Give him/her a small spoon or two of food and then finish the meal with more breastmilk or formula milk if necessary. Your baby will become frustrated with solid food if it is given when they are very hungry.

It is vital to get accustomed to the method of eating like sitting up straight and eating food from a spoon. Let the baby rest after each spoonful and stop feeding them when they are full. These early experiences can help your babies to learn sensible consumption habits throughout their lives.

Do not be surprised if most of the first solid-food feedings end up on the baby's face, bib, and hands! Increase the quantity of food step by step with simply a teaspoon or 2 at the start. This will help a baby to learn the way to swallow food.

If the baby cries or avoids food when you feed him/her, don't pressurize the baby to eat. Return to bottle-feeding or breast-feeding completely for a time before attempting again. Keep in mind that starting solid foods is a gradual process. Initially, your baby will still obtain most of his nutrition from breast-feeding, formula milk, or both. Also, every baby is different, therefore, each baby will be ready for solid food at a different time.

If parents want to make their own baby food rather than purchasing it, they can use a food processor, blender, or just mash the food with the help of a spoon or fork and sieve. Fresh foods should be cooked properly without adding any salt or seasoning. Bananas and avocados are soft and need no cooking, so you can easily give them to babies by mashing them. Other fruits and vegetables can be cooked well until they are soft and can easily be swallowed by babies. If you refrigerate the food and after 1 or 2 days you are giving it to your little ones, first check the food if it is spoiled, because fresh foods can spoil more quickly as compared to the jarred/canned foods. Freezing small portions in ice cube trays is a good way to keep home-made baby food fresh.

Do remember to give a good variety of foods that are healthy and rich in nutrients and can fulfill the baby's needs. Do not overfeed them.

ALLERGENIC FOODS

It is suggested that you feed your babies potentially allergenic foods together with other compatible, previously tried foods. These foods are:

- Egg
- Dairy products
- Peanuts and tree nuts
- Soy
- Fish

There is no proof that a delay in starting such foods will assist in preventing food allergies. In reality, timely introduction of foods containing peanuts, for example, may lessen the danger that your baby will have a peanut allergy.

SUGGESTED BABY FOODS BY THEIR AGE

Pediatricians suggest certain baby foods for certain ages. It is very important to introduce a variety of foods (fruits, vegetables, meat) so that they can get used to different tastes and begin to get a variety of nutrients.

Four to six months

- Mainly formula milk or breastmilk
- Pureed fruit (peaches, apples, bananas)
- Pureed cooked vegetables (squash, peas)
- Pureed meat (chicken, beef)
- Semi liquid, iron-fortified cereals (select a cereal that is made of oats and barley and avoid rice cereals)

How much to give:

- Start with a very small amount of single-ingredient pureed food. Give one or half a teaspoon.
- Slowly increase the amount to 1 to 2 tablespoons.
- If you are giving cereal, mix it with formula milk or breastmilk and not cow's milk.

Six to eight months

- Mainly formula milk or breastmilk
- Strained or unsweetened pureed fruits (pears, banana, avocado, peaches, applesauce)
- Pureed or strained vegetables (sweet potato, squash, well-cooked carrots)
- Pureed or mashed meat (chicken, beef)
- Mashed or pureed tofu
- Small pieces of bread
- Pureed or mashed legumes (kidney beans, lentils, chickpeas, black beans)

How much to give:

- Fruits: 2 to 3 tablespoons. Slowly increase it to 4 to 8 tablespoons.
- Vegetables: 2 to 3 tablespoons. Slowly increase it to 4 to 8 tablespoons.
- Grain products: 1 to 2 tablespoons. Slowly increase it to 2 to 4 tablespoons.
- Protein-rich foods: 1 to 2 tablespoons. Slowly increase it to 2 to 4 tablespoons.

Eight to twelve months

- Formula milk or breastmilk
- Unsweetened yogurt, soft pasteurized cheese, and cottage cheese
- Soft cooked, bite-size vegetables (potatoes, sweet potatoes, squash, carrots)
- Mashed or cut into soft cubes or strips of fruits (pears, avocados, bananas, peaches)
- Finger foods (tiny bits of scrambled eggs, well-cooked potatoes, teething crackers, O-shaped cereals. Avoid sugared, processed cereals and cookies.)
- Foods rich in proteins (small bits of boneless fish, meat, chicken, tofu, well-cooked beans like lentils, split peas, or black beans)
- Iron-fortified cereals (wheat, barley, oats, mixed cereals)

How much to give:

- Fruits: Half or ¾ cup
- Vegetables: Half or ¾ cup
- Grain products: ¼ or a half cup
- Protein-rich foods: ¼ s or a half cup

SOME SOLID FOODS TO AVOID

Some foods are not recommended for babies until their proper age. These foods are:

- **Honey:** Avoid giving honey to babies before 12 months because it comes with a risk of botulism.
- **Cow's milk:** Try not to give cow's milk to infants until

they are 1 year old. Use breastmilk or formula milk for feeding and mixing in cereal etc.

- **Choking hazards:** Avoid foods that are the cause of choking hazards. Such food includes seeds, raisins, nuts, hard candies, hard raw vegetables, grapes, peanut butter, hot dogs, and popcorn.

MILK SELECTION AND FOODS FOR YOUR TODDLER

*N*utrition and foods for toddlers work the same as that for adults. With a growing body and bones, your toddler needs all the important nutrients like protein, calcium, vitamins, minerals, carbohydrates, and fats. Of course, the amount of these nutrients needed is different for toddlers and adults.

Your toddler is now ready to eat any type of solid food because his teeth are grown and he can chew anything. Don't hesitate to introduce a variety of foods to your toddler. You can, and should, give him almost anything that you are making for the whole family. Highly spiced foods may not be tolerated at this age.

The selection of milk sometimes becomes a big question and struggle for parents. Milk for your babies must contain vitamins like D, B6, B12, A, and B3. It should also have a sufficient number of proteins, fats, calcium, potassium, phosphorus, etc.

I am here to share my experience with the selection of milk for my first baby. I will discuss this later in this chapter.

SOME NUTRIENTS ARE A MUST

Your toddler needs the nutrients contained in these foods:

- **Fruits:** Make sure your baby gets into the habit of eating fruits every day from the very start of their solid food journey. You can use fresh or canned fruits to give your baby. However, be careful of the fruits canned in heavy sugar syrups. Choose the varieties canned in natural, unsweetened fruit juice. Fruit juices are also an option but make sure if you are giving your baby juices, they should be 100% juice without any artificial flavor and sugars. Remember though that even 100% fruit juice is full of natural sugars (fructose) and should preferably be diluted with water. Give these in moderation and rather give your toddler whole fresh fruits.

Dried fruits make good snacks.

- **Vegetables:** Second to fruits, vegetables are the best source of nutrients for your baby. You can try fresh or frozen vegetables with or without cooking. Be careful of canned veg as they often contain a lot of salt. Vegetables including green, orange, or red colors are good options to start with.
- **Proteins:** I have been vegan for 9 years but as I am here to tell you everything about feeding your baby, I will also suggest some protein-rich non-vegan foods for your baby. Lean meat, poultry, and eggs are options for non-vegan mamas. Beans, peas, soy products, and nuts are good options for protein-rich foods for vegan and non-vegans alike.
- **Dairy:** Try to develop a habit in your baby to eat and

drink dairy milk products because they have calcium and other minerals needed for baby's growth. . Milk is the best option with others being unflavored, unsweetened yogurt, cheese, and soy beverages. When serving yogurt, you can add some stewed fruit, fresh fruit, or cinnamon for sweetness.

WHAT TO AVOID IN TODDLER FOODS

- Added sugars
- Artificial flavors
- Trans and saturated fats
- Sodium
- Candies, cookies, and processed foods
- Slippery fruits like whole grapes
- Hard foods
- Sticky foods
- Foods your baby is allergic to

MILK MATTERS

Milk is the most important part of the diet of your toddler especially for the first 10-12 months. It is the best source of calcium (needed for bone growth) and Vitamin D (needed for bones and muscle development). The recommended amount of calcium and Vitamin D for toddlers is

- 700 mg calcium/day
- 600 IU vitamin D/day

Babies between 1-2 years should be given whole milk (two servings a day) to fulfill their dietary needs. These are needed for their normal body and brain growth. However, if your baby is overweight and you have a family history of obesity, you should consult a nutritionist who will suggest low-fat milk or some alternative for it.

There are dairy and non-dairy kinds of milk available for your toddler. It is up to you and your baby's nutritionist to select which milk you want for your baby.

TYPES OF MILK FOR TODDLERS

When it comes to introducing milk to your baby other than breastmilk, you'll find plenty of options. You can select what is best for your child and which milk suits your baby's stomach. For my first child, we used soy milk but after much research, we switched to hemp milk.

Following are the common kinds of milk for toddlers:

- **Whole cows' milk**

This milk is a very common option for toddler milk in many countries. Cows' milk, when mixed with other foods, makes an excellent option for toddlers' milk. It has a sufficient amount of calcium, vitamin D, protein, fats, phosphorus, etc.

Some babies reject whole cows' milk due to its very different taste from breastmilk. Some mamas don't choose dairy milk as an option for their babies because it contains extra fats and more lactose which sometimes can cause a problem with babies, especially those who are overweight.

- **Hemp milk**

Hemp milk has more calories, protein, and carbohydrates than cow's milk. It contains more protein and healthy fats than other plant-based milk substitutes. Unlike other non-dairy milk choices, hemp milk is composed of all the vital amino acids, making it a whole protein.

The fat present in hemp milk is unsaturated and has omega-3 and omega-6 fatty acids. These amino acids are vital for growth and you can only get them in foods because your body doesn't make them.

Hemp milk is also a good source of vitamin A, calcium, vitamin D, vitamin B12, iron, phosphorus, and zinc.

- **Soy milk**

Soy milk is just like whole cows' milk as it contains almost the same nutrients. It is the most recommended plant source of milk for babies. This is best for babies who are allergic to cows' milk and goats' milk. This milk provides fortified vitamin D and calcium in sufficient amounts.

Among other options, you can introduce your babies to

- Oat milk (has fewer proteins than soy and hemp milk)
- Coconut milk (higher iron content)
- Goats' milk

SOME FOOD RECIPES FOR YOUR TODDLER

You can give most eatables to your toddler unless he is allergic to them. Toddlers tend to eat new things with enthusiasm and they want a variety of tastes every day. There are plenty of options for making meals for your toddlers but here are some common and simple recipes I would like to share with you.

1. Carrot, Orange, and Mango Lollies

This is a delicious, juicy treat for your toddlers. It is great for soothing sore, teething gums.

Ingredients:

- 50 g carrots
- 1 orange
- 150 g mango

All of them peeled and chopped well

- 100 ml apple juice

How to make it:

- Put all the ingredients into a blender or food processor.
- Run it until the ingredients are smooth and thin.
- Take this smoothie out and pour it into lolly-shaped ice molds.
- Freeze for 5 hours and they are good to go.

1. Veggie Frittata Muffins

This is a delicious recipe for families who don't eat meat

Ingredients:

- 100 g broccoli
- 65 g tinned sweetcorn
- 2-3 eggs
- 2 tbsp milk
- 50 g cheddar cheese, grated
- 4 onions, chopped

How to make it:

- Preheat the oven to 180°C.
- Steam the broccoli for 4-5 minutes. Refresh under cold water and chop.
- Put the eggs in a bowl. Add milk and beat well.
- Add broccoli, corn, and onions to the bowl.
- Spoon the mixture into greased muffin pans, filling them ¾ of the way.
- Bake for 20-25 minutes until the mixture sets. Wait till the color changes to golden.
- Serve warm

1. Roasted Squash

This is one of my favorite things to give my babies. They love these roasted squashes especially if I make them in different fun shapes.

Ingredients:

- Squashes
- Olive oil
- Maple syrup
- Cinnamon
- Rosemary to serve

How to make it:

- Take a big bowl and add squash cut into different fun shapes (you can use different tools like cookie-cutters to cut it into different shapes for your baby).
- Add a little olive oil, maple syrup, and spices to the bowl.
- Toss everything around to coat the squash.
- Spread the squash onto baking sheets. Every piece of

squash should be separated.
- Place the baking sheets in the oven for 15-20 minutes at 400°F. Take the sheets out and turn every piece of squash over.
- Bake for another 15 minutes. The delicious roasted squash is ready.
- For further taste, sprinkle fresh chopped rosemary on them.

1. Mac and Cheese Zucchini Spirals

This is a very healthy dish for your toddlers and it has very low carbs. My babies love to eat this dish.

Ingredients:

- 1 or 2 tbsp. olive oil
- 2 small or medium spiralized zucchini
- Small piece of butter (1 tbsp.)
- 1 tbsp. of all-purpose flour
- 1 small cup of shredded cheddar cheese
- ¼ tbsp mustard powder
- ½ cup cream
- ¼ tbsp chili powder
- Salt to taste

How to make it:

- Heat the olive oil in a skillet and add zucchini noodles. Cook until tender but still crisp.
- Turn off the heat, drain zucchini, and pat dry.
- Melt the butter at medium heat in a saucepan and add

flour and stir until it becomes smooth.

- Now add cream, cheese, mustard, and chili powder one by one to the saucepan.
- Beat and stir until the sauce is thick and smooth and the cheese is melted. Taste and add salt if you think it's needed.
- Add zucchini noodles to this cheese sauce and mix well. When coated properly with sauce, the dish is ready to be eaten.

Other foods that you can make at home for toddlers

- Chicken and apple balls
- Bake chicken nuggets
- French toast sticks
- Honey roasted carrots
- Vegan arancini
- Avocado and black bean
- Unsweetened yogurt with sliced berries
- Vegetable and chicken soups
- Banana pancakes (mix 1 ripe banana, 1 egg, and 2 tbsp. wheat flour. Cook 3-4 minutes on each side over average heat)

HOW TO MAKE BABY FOOD

*B*reastfeeding is recommended as the only food for your baby till he is 6 months old and is ready to eat solids. Breastfeeding, along with solid foods, should be continued till the baby becomes two years old (sometimes mamas settle for one year only). The best time to introduce solids to your baby is when he turns 6 months old.

Many mamas get confused about the following things:

- What solid foods should I start giving my baby first?
- Should I buy ready-made baby food?
- Should I make food for my baby at home?
- Which foods can be made at home?
- How will I make solid foods for my baby?
- What utensils should I use to make baby food?

Being a mama of three, all these questions ran through my mind every time I wanted to make my baby start solid foods. I worked hard and learned everything about making baby food at home. To me, homemade baby food is best because you can make it hygienically, you can trust what ingredients you're putting into it, it's cheaper, and you can make it fresh.

I have always loved making food for my young ones. I have worked through all the challenges a mama will face in making baby foods and I am here to share my experience to guide you to be able to make baby foods at home with ease and satisfaction.

Baby foods should contain all the nutrients, minerals, and components essential for your baby so that your baby would not fall into any deficiencies. So, mamas, you have to keep a keen eye on this aspect of baby foods. You can consult a baby nutritionist for this and get help from other mamas about what foods are necessary for your baby.

WHY I PREFER HOMEMADE BABY FOOD

If you are going to make homemade food for your baby, you will have a greater number of options and can make food rich in more nutrients. You can choose fruits and vegetables for your baby and can store them for further use at home so you don't have to go to the market every day.

Homemade foods allow babies to have a wide range of flavors and it will develop a habit in your baby for braver eating. You can control the amount of sugar and salt in homemade foods which allows you to make the taste your baby loves without adding unhealthy amounts of these things.

I am not a master chef but I am good at making food for my babies as it is not that difficult or technical. You just need to have a little knowledge about how to make baby food which I'm here to tell you. On the other hand, foods available in the market lose their important nutrients while being processed and packed food are sometimes not safe for babies. Market foods lose their yumminess which you can provide your baby by making food at home, fresh and rich in nutrients. I prefer homemade baby foods for many reasons:

- I know what and how many nutrients I'm feeding my baby.
- It is cheaper than processed food available on the market.
- My baby gets pure, tasty, fresh food.
- Every choice is my own to make, selecting, making, and serving baby foods.
- My babies learned to try different textured and flavored foods.

IT IS super easy to make baby foods at home. Manufacturers of commercial foods process the foods at very high temperatures to kill bacteria and other pathogens for longer storage in cans which at the same time also destroys important nutrients in the food.

I just needed one day of working to make baby food for the next complete week and storage was super easy. I would process fruits and vegetables in a food blender and make purees. Or I would steam vegetables or meat. I stored the baby food for just 5-7 days.

Making baby food at home is the best thing to do related to the diet and health of your baby. Let me tell you how to get started in making baby food and master it in just a few days.

GETTING STARTED WITH MAKING BABY FOOD

Any mom who wants to start preparing food for her baby might find it difficult to start. Begin with little steps and simple foods. Try making banana or avocado puree by just mashing them in a bowl till they become smooth. This is a very good step to start making food for your baby.

After a good response from your baby, you will get motivation and now you can move to a bigger step to make nutrient-rich foods that are not very common. You can prepare beets, broccoli, turnips, asparagus, spinach, kale, mango and papaya purees for your baby.

Boil and mash the food well before offering it to your baby. Give your baby only one new food at a time and keep on introducing new foods after a few days. Use things available according to the season and do not add any type of salt, sugars, or flavors.

In the start, your baby will only need 1 or 2 spoons to satisfy his hunger. So, make sure you only make small amounts of food at a time. Look out for allergies in your baby. Your baby might get allergies from some specific thing in his food. Once you know, avoid them. Common allergic foods may be peanuts, wheat, fish, and soy.

There is no proper order of introducing foods to a baby, you can start with anything you want. Making baby food should be taken as fun so that you enjoy making it and it won't become a burden.

My whole family is vegan so I'll not recommend any food related to meat for babies as I haven't ever made them. However, I can tell you about non-vegan foods – you can try them if you are not strictly vegan. Other than fruits and vegetables you can also use a puree of meat (properly cooked with no pink spots left). Remember to remove any skin, the fat layer, and the layer of connective tissue from meat as these are hard for a baby's little stomach to digest.

EQUIPMENT YOU NEED FOR MAKING BABY FOOD

Making food for babies does not require you to be a master chef. Similarly, it doesn't require you to have fancy or expensive types of equipment. You can go with traditional methods for making food. A simple food processor or blender can be enough to make food purees and mashed solids. But still, according to my experience as a mama, here is a list of things you'll find useful for making baby food:

- Bowl, steamer basket, or electric steamer
- Blender or simple food processor
- Cutting board
- Good knife
- An immersion blender (if available or needed)
- Pure, clean water
- Ice storage trays or cups
- Storage bowls
- Baking sheets
- Baby spoons and bowls in bright colors (my baby girl was more attracted to brightly colored spoons and bowls)
- Freezer bags for storage
- An all-in-one baby food processor which steams, cooks, and purees baby food in a single go (only if you can afford it and don't have any other choice)
- A chair with a front desk attached to it where you can place food in front of the baby (high chair).
- A large number of wipes (you'll need them in bulk!)

When you have everything needed for making baby food, you are good to go. One important thing I want you to remember before starting making baby food is always make your food well mashed, smooth, and thin, as new eaters don't have teeth or proper swallowing techniques. As the baby grows older you can start making thicker, lumpier food for him. To make baby food thin and smooth you need to add water or breastmilk in it every time. Try adding the cooking water from the fruit or vegetables for extra nutrients and flavor.

SIMPLE 6-STEP PROCEDURE FOR MAKING BABY FOOD

Although there are many techniques and procedures for making baby food, let me start with a common and easy 6-step procedure that helped me to be quick and expert in making baby food.

1. Wash your hands, tools, and food prep area.
2. After properly washing fruits and vegetables, peel them accurately. Remove any seeds or pits as they are harder for the baby to digest.
3. Either steam, boil, bake, roast, or microwave the food until it becomes smooth (microwaving and steaming are best as they preserve most of the vital nutrients).
4. Use a blender or food processor to make a puree of the food by adding a small amount of liquid (it can be sterilized water, breastmilk, or formula milk). If you don't have a blender, rub the food through a sieve. You can also simply mash the food when your baby becomes older and can go with more texture.
5. Put the food your baby will eat for one meal into his favorite bowl. Use his favorite spoon and you are good to go.

6. Store any extra food in small freezer bags, cups, or covered ice trays for future use. Rewarm the food to a lukewarm temperature.

STAGE 1 BABY FOODS

All the foods you will make for your baby when he first starts eating solids will fall under Stage 1 baby foods. These foods are mostly thin and smooth and easy for the baby to handle with his toothless mouth.

Stage 1 foods consist of simple fruit and vegetable purees. Try to make small quantities of food at this stage because the baby will be full after just 1-2 spoonfuls.

STAGE 2 BABY FOODS

These foods are more complex than Stage 1 foods. These may have 2 or 3 ingredients in puree form. These allow the baby to have a wider range of tastes and textures as he is growing. Most mamas start Stage 2 baby foods when their baby is 7-8 months old. These foods are thicker and less smooth because now the baby has developed a habit of chewing foods as some of his teeth have come through.

For me, there were no such stages of food. I just went with my instinct and did not follow the calendar. I just made whatever I found best for my baby and it was a big success.

HOW TO BLEND BABY FOODS

Hey, mamas! Making baby foods at home is a simple process but you'll need a little practice to become good at it. You need proper practice and a good hand in making the food smooth, thin, and creamy. Blending is most important for the baby who has just started eating solids. Blending can be less important once the baby has grown up and his teeth have come out.

Tips for blending baby food

- **Give it time:** Don't rush while blending food. Give your blender some time to run and make food smoother. The average time that a blender takes to blend the food to smoothness is 1-2 minutes. This time can be longer with older blenders or food processors.
- **Add liquids:** Ingredients for the baby food do not become properly smooth until some liquid is added to them. You can use pumped breastmilk, formula milk, or some water to liquefy the puree. Add this liquid into the blender or food processor and then run it. The amount of liquid depends upon the nature of the food you are blending. Some vegetables and fruits take up more liquid than others. I mostly use ¼ cup or less to make smooth puree for my baby. Don't add more water or it will make a runny puree.
- **Cyclone effect:** This is a visual aid that tells you whether you have an adequate amount of liquid and solid in the blender. If the amounts are right, all the things in the blender will move in a completely circular motion without interruptions making a cyclone effect.
- **Change the sides:** When the blender is running, make sure to change the sides of ingredients in the puree with a spatula so that they mix well.
- **Food processor vs high-speed blender:** A food processor is great but it makes slightly thicker purees than a blender. On the other hand, the blender has a higher speed and makes thinner, smoother purees. A

food processor requires less liquid to make a puree than a blender.

HOW TO STORE/FREEZE BABY FOOD

The best thing about making your own baby food is that you can store it in the freezer. You can make enough for a week or two and then store it for later use. You can safely freeze your baby food for up to 3 months without much nutrient loss.

Whenever you make any baby food, your baby won't finish the whole thing in just one day. Store the remaining purees in the refrigerator for up to 3-4 days so that your baby can enjoy them again. However, don't store anything that's left in the plate you've fed the baby from. The enzymes in his saliva will cause the food to become watery. Remember to put the purees of baby foods into the refrigerator within two hours of cooking to prevent germ growth. Here's the simple procedure of freezing and storing baby foods;

- Make the puree and let it cool at room temperature.
- Put the puree into freezing trays or bowls.
- Make sure to cover the freezing trays or bowls with the lid.
- Do not forget to label them with the date and name of the puree on the tray or bowl.
- Put the tray or bowl into the freezer for 5-6 hours till it gets fully frozen.
- Take the tray or bowl out when the puree is completely frozen and crack the puree out.
- Put the frozen puree into baggies with zip locks and store for up to 3 months.

Most purees can be kept in the fridge for 3-4 days. My recommendation is to use the stored purees within 3 days.

HOW TO DEFROST BABY FOODS

Defrosting the frozen baby foods looks easy but it can be hard sometimes. Baby foods can be defrosted in the following ways;

- **Microwave:** This is the most common and easy way to thaw baby food. Put the frozen food in a glass container in the microwave. Run the microwave for 20 seconds intervals with stirring after every 20 seconds (this way, it will evenly warm not leaving any cold or extremely hot spots).

Feel the temperature of the puree by touching it and you'll know it is warm enough to take it out of the microwave. I always taste the puree before giving it to my baby. In this way, I get to check the taste and texture of the puree (whether it still tastes good or not), and also, I get to know the temperature of the food.

- **Stovetop:** This is also an easy and convenient way to defrost baby food. Take a very small saucepan and put it on the stove on medium heat. Put the frozen puree and heat until it becomes smooth and warm. Remember to stir at regular intervals.
- **Warm water bowl:** This is a traditional and simple technique to thaw baby foods. I use it most of the time and find it easier than the other methods. Take a bowl full of medium warm water and put the frozen bag puree in it and let it remain for a few minutes. The puree will defrost to a lukewarm temperature.

PUREES I MADE FOR MY BABIES

As I discussed earlier simple recipes of making purees, most of these purees are made in the same way. The difference is in the addition of liquid and the cooking process of food. Here are some purees I made for my babies with proper age division:

For babies 5 to 6 months old

1. Banana puree
2. Avocado puree
3. Pea/green bean puree
4. Brown rice cereals
5. Baked sweet potato puree
6. First carrot puree

For babies 7 to 9 months old

1. Pumpkin thyme puree
2. First spinach with white thyme
3. Beet and blueberry mash
4. Avocado and banana baby food
5. Veggies and sole puree
6. Papaya puree
7. Butternut squash and pear puree

For babies 9 to 12 months old

1. Whitefish and leek puree
2. Quinoa Ratatouille
3. Baby beef stew
4. Mix fruit puree (blueberries, mango, and avocado)
5. Quinoa banana mash
6. Creamy Provencal chicken

7. Minted Greek and cherry yogurt food puree
8. Banana and apricot puree

For babies over 12 months old

1. Mixed fruits with added spices food puree
2. Yogurt and milk
3. Whole-grain pancakes
4. Boiled or fried eggs
5. Chicken and turkey bites

Most babies, when they become more than 12 months old, will start eating anything made for the family. There are so many other options of baby foods and you can improvise anything you like for your babies. Hey, mamas! Let us start making homemade baby food for our babies.

TIPS AND TRICKS FOR GETTING YOUR BABY TO EAT SOLIDS

*H*ey, mama! Your baby has grown and now he is 6-7 months old. You should by now have started giving him foods like fruits and vegetables as well as breastmilk. A growing baby's body not only needs nutrients from breastmilk but also other healthy foods to meet its needs.

You are happy because now you can try things other than breastmilk. Rice cereals and fruits are considered to be the best foods for a baby who is just starting to eat solids but any healthy food is good for your baby when he is 6 months old.

Sometimes it is difficult to introduce foods other than breastmilk to the baby because he has only developed a taste for breastmilk. Some babies refuse new tastes and don't want anything except breastmilk but as the baby needs those foods for his development, mamas become worried about what to do to make their babies eat new foods like fruits and purees.

IT IS A SUPER-FOOD

Vegetables and fruits mostly used as food for infants contain many nutrients like vitamins, proteins, carbohydrates, and minerals. On the other hand, breastmilk is a natural source of antioxidants, antibodies, enzymes, and other healthy components necessary for the baby.

These together are everything your baby needs to grow up healthily. Mixing both can make "SUPER-FOOD".

Combining these superfoods makes a great snack for your baby. There are a lot of recipes and ways to make purees and mixed foods of fruits or vegetables and breastmilk. I'll tell you about the ones I used to feed my baby and believe me these are so good and healthy.

The transition from breastmilk to solids is a very delicate process and it should be well managed otherwise it can cause problems for mamas and babies. Many mamas start worrying about finding ways of introducing solids to their babies.

Don't worry, mama, I'm here to tell you a wonderful solution for this tension. You can mix your breastmilk with solid foods and fruits to give the baby a familiar taste plus something new.

Yes! That's right, you can mix a few ounces of breastmilk with the solids you want to give your baby and can make a puree with solid food and breastmilk. This will help the transition from breastmilk to solids go smoothly and easily. As foods will have a taste of breastmilk in them, the baby will easily eat them.

HOW MUCH BREASTMILK YOU SHOULD USE FOR MIXING

You can use pumped milk and can even store it in the refrigerator. Remember not to add a lot of breastmilk into solids. 1-2 ounces are enough to develop a taste of breastmilk in the foods.

Stored breastmilk can go bad if stored for too many days. Enzymes present in breastmilk can alter the taste and texture of milk stored in the refrigerator for too long. On the other hand, you cannot pump 1-2 ounces every time before giving food to the baby. So, pump the amount of breastmilk that's enough for 2 or 3 days.

WAYS TO USE BREASTMILK IN FOODS FOR BABIES

Breastmilk can be mixed with almost every food you are introducing to your baby. There are 3 main ways to do so.

1. Breastmilk into baby cereals

This is the most common and convenient way of mixing breastmilk into foods. Cereals are quick and basic solid foods for your baby and mixing your breastmilk into them makes them healthier. Here is the basic recipe:

- Put 2-3 spoons of baby cereal into a bowl.
- Add 1-2 ounces of fresh or frozen breastmilk.
- Stir it well to mix it properly and you are good to go.

You can add breastmilk to any type of baby cereal. Sometimes you have to use warm milk to make the cereal. Remember not to boil or microwave breastmilk because it will destroy all the important nutrients and enzymes in it. Rather, hold the breast-milk container under running warm water or place the container in a bowl containing warm water for just 1 or 2 minutes.

1. Breastmilk into milk smoothies

When you start giving solids to your baby, milk smoothies become a very good option for baby food and if you add breast-milk when making smoothies, they become the richest food for your baby. You can make smoothies from fruits. Here is how it is done:

- Take fruit or vegetable puree for baby
- Add a small amount of breastmilk to it (fresh or frozen)
- Blend it in a blender until it becomes smooth
- Ready to serve

These breastmilk smoothies are the best source of baby food in hot summers. You can serve them in your baby's favorite cup.

1. Breastmilk into purees

THE TRANSITION from boob to food is always a deliberate and time-taking process for the baby. The easiest way to do this transition is to mix breastmilk with baby food purees. I have experienced that babies easily accept new foods if they contain a familiar taste.

I used this technique with all my three babies and it was a great success. Every mama out there should try it and introducing solids to your baby will become very easy and smooth. I used every kind of puree recommended for babies. I gave them alone first and tried them with mixing the breastmilk, believe me, the combination of purees and breastmilk was a great success and I'm really glad that I found it this way. You can make breastmilk puree in three steps;

STEP **1**

Take few ounces (Recommended 1-2) of fresh or stored milk in the cup or bowl your baby likes the most.

STEP **2**

Pour the puree you made with baby's favorite fruit (you can also buy them) into to the bowl and softly mix it.

STEP **3**

Keep on mixing till it becomes smooth. One of the best baby food puree is ready to serve.

MY BABY'S FAVORITE HOMEMADE PUREES AND THEIR RECIPES

Like every mama out there I also had to try different purees for my baby until I selected a few of the best. These purees are best because they contain essential nutrients important for babies to have in the early few months. Mixing breastmilk in these purees made my life easier and my baby became fond of them.

Here are some of the breastmilk purees and their recipes that worked best for me and I hope they will work for every mama:

1. Avocado-breastmilk puree

This is one of the best first foods for babies. Avocados have an enjoyable taste and contain a great number of vitamins and beneficial oils. This puree is super easy to make because no cooking is needed for it.

- Peel the avocado and cut it into small pieces.
- Take one or two pieces and mash them in a bowl.
- Add breastmilk while mashing the fruit.
- When properly mashed and mixed, feed the baby with a soft, small spoon.

At the start, use a very small piece of avocado and use more milk so your baby will easily take it. Gradually keep on increasing the amount of avocado and decreasing the amount of breastmilk. Always offer small bites to a baby who is new to eating solids. Your little one only needs one or 2 spoons of food to satisfy his hunger. You can store the puree in the fridge and use it later.

1. Green bean and breastmilk puree

Green beans are a good source of vitamins, fiber, and calcium. They are great for babies from 6 months to 2-3 years old. If you start giving them to your baby at the very start, they will get used to it. For making this puree:

- Properly wash green beans which you can easily buy from the market.
- Cook the beans in a steamer for 3 to 5 minutes until soft. Run cold water over them.
- Blend the beans in a blender or food processor until they become a smooth puree.
- While blending, add a few ounces of your breastmilk and mix well.
- The perfect side meal is ready for your baby.

Green beans are one of the favorite sources of food for my babies and all the mamas should try them. This will become a permanent part of your baby food menu.

SWEET POTATO AND BREASTMILK PUREE

Sweet potato is one of the best foods which is first introduced to a baby especially in the form of puree. They are full of nutrients and easily available. They have been used as the first food for babies for generations. They are naturally sweet and soft so make wonderful baby food. For making this puree:

- Take 1 or 2 sweet potatoes, peel, and wash them.
- Steam the sweet potatoes for 20 to 25 minutes until very soft.
- Blend or puree them in a high-speed blender or food processor until they become a smooth paste.
- Add a few (1 or 2) ounces of breastmilk and mix.
- It is ready to be enjoyed by mama's little angel.

Sweet potatoes are very common and cheap. They can be stored at room temperature for many weeks. Don't use them as daily food because they can cause gas allergies to your babies (in very rare cases when not digested properly).

1. Banana-breastmilk puree

Bananas are a wonderful first food for a baby as they are already soft and mushy and they are pretty easy to digest. Bananas are packed full of vitamins and minerals. Banana puree can be in just 1 minute.

- Take a fully ripe banana and peel it.
- Gently smash it with a spoon in a bowl.
- Add a few ounces of breastmilk and it is ready to be enjoyed by your baby.

Like bananas, you can make puree from any other fruit and add breastmilk to it to give your baby an excellent range of healthy foods.

Fruits are a good source of nutrients for a baby and when they are given with breastmilk, this combination becomes everything that the body of your baby needs to grow and it also helps in bone building.

ADDING breastmilk in starting foods for your baby will help him develop the habit of eating solids and he will start liking it. You can gradually keep on decreasing the amount of breastmilk in foods as your baby is growing fond of these fruits and cereals.

Because you will not keep on producing breastmilk, one day your baby will have to eat these foods without your breastmilk. So, make sure you transition your baby from breastmilk foods to foods without breastmilk over a few months.

STORING PUMPED MILK

As mama is going to use breastmilk in foods for her babies, she cannot sit and pump her breast before every meal because babies usually eat 3-5 times a day. Luckily, breastmilk can be stored in a refrigerator for a few days.

You should pump the amount of milk needed for 3-5 days and store it frozen in food jars. Storing in food jars gave me a solution to milk getting wasted and becoming sour. Frozen breastmilk in food jars is easy to use. Just place the jar in a bowl full of warm water and let it remain for a while. Once breastmilk has thawed and become slightly warm, use it to make baby food.

- **At room temperature**: Breastmilk can be stored at room temperature for a maximum of 4-6 hours depending upon the temperature. Don't let it remain unrefrigerated in the kitchen for too long.
- **In the insulated cooler:** Breastmilk can be stored in a well-insulated cooler with ice packets in it for a maximum of 24 hours. This is very useful when you are going on family trips and picnics.
- **In the refrigerator:** Freshly pumped milk can be stored in the refrigerator for a maximum of 4-6 days. However, I recommend not storing it for more than three days. It may lose its texture and taste due to enzyme action.
- **In a deep freeze:** Breastmilk can be stored in a deep freeze for up to 10-12 months but it is recommended to use it within 6 months.

Hey mamas! Keep in mind that the longer you store breastmilk, the greater the chance of losing vitamin K and important enzymes. Remember to store breastmilk in small batches.

* * *

Leave a 1-Click Review!

Customer Reviews

⭐⭐⭐⭐⭐ 2

5.0 out of 5 stars ▾

5 star		100%
4 star		0%
3 star		0%
2 star		0%
1 star		0%

Share your thoughts with other customers

Write a customer review

See all verified purchase reviews ›

AT THIS POINT, I would be incredibly thankful if you could just take 60 seconds to write a brief review on Amazon about how this book has helped you thus far, even if it's just a few sentences! I will love to read them all!

AFTERWORD

Excellent! It was a great journey writing this book. As it is finally finished, I am feeling spectacular about it. Although it was a tiresome two months of writing this book, believe me the end is completely worth the struggle. I had to stay at my writing desk for long hours through day and night along with handling my three babies. Sometimes, I had to stay up all night to write chapters of this book. There was a time when I got exhausted with it but then I remembered why I started it in the first place i.e. to bring positive change in the lives of many mothers. That was my motivation and strength to keep on writing this book for all the mothers like me out there.

Remember, I am writing this book as a mother of three. Every sentence of this book contains the life experiences I faced during feeding my babies from day one till they were 2 years old. Being inexperienced at first, it was hard to cope with the procedures involved in feeding a baby but with continued struggle and learning I found my way in and it was a wonderful experience. In this book, I have written everything a mama needs to know about feeding her baby.

Babies are a very delicate and sensitive part of our lives and similarly taking care of them is a sensitive matter. Inexperience can result in disturbances for mama and the baby. But not every mother needs to be born with this experience because this is something 100% learnable and that is what I have tried in this book. I have tried to cover every step of feeding and handling your babies including breastfeeding, bottle feeding, making solid foods, etc.

Learning these things is not tough but it does take time and perseverance. You cannot learn everything about feeding your baby in a day or two. It took me three babies to become an experienced mama and then I decided to write this book for you so that every new mama can learn from my experience and become a supermom more quickly. If you have read my whole book, you will know that I'm not exaggerating anything here.

You need to keep in mind that you are the only one who has to take care of your baby, feed him, cook for him, pamper him and make him comfortable in any way possible. This is a must-do job for every mother and she needs to be ready for everything if she wants a happy and healthy motherhood. Many mamas think of motherhood as a challenge but actually, it is something worth experiencing. Though it has both pros and cons, believe me handling and feeding your young is the best thing in the world to do. You get so much peace and satisfaction when your baby smiles at you because his mama has done it well for him.

Sometimes a mama has to choose options other than breast-feeding like bottle feeding. Bottle feeding is also a learnable technique and it should be done correctly to avoid nipple confusion and breast refusal. In this book, you have learned everything about bottle feeding, some of the best ways and techniques for it. Newborns take time to learn everything. Along with bottle feeding comes formula milk and I have shared my experience in selecting the best formula milk for your baby and how to use it. Formula milk should have essential nutrients needed for your baby's growth and development.

Besides everything about feeding a baby, I have again and again talked about your health both physically and mentally. Remember that only a healthy mama can raise a healthy child. So you need to take care of yourself by any means possible. Keep yourself well managed and try to stay out of stress. I have experienced that all we mamas want for our babies is for them to grow up healthy and have sufficient of everything. By handling this sometimes we forget to take care of ourselves and some physical and mental conditions kick in. Try to eat healthily and stay stress-free because a mama is very susceptible to falling into mental issues due to increasing pressure and stress.

I have repeatedly written in this book that you are the only master and authority when it comes to feeding your baby. You don't need to rush into the things you cannot manage or are difficult for you. Always try to find an easy and relaxing way so that you and your baby remain comfortable in every situation. You have to make decisions for feeding your baby. Don't be afraid to try new things while making food for your baby. Young ones like to have new tastes every day. Be creative with everything and shape the baby food into fun shapes so it would attract your baby to eat.

Last, but not least, I wrote this book for every mama out there. Stop feeling yourself as a failure mama if you have done 1 or 2 things wrong in feeding your baby. That happens to all of us. All that matters is that we keep on trying for the sake of the health and growth of our babies. Many times, I also thought of giving up on this but something inside, which is called motherhood, kept me going and I succeeded in becoming a better mama for my babies. You are lucky that there is someone to guide you about what to do. This book is all about guiding you to become able to handle everything with feeding your babies and getting out of tiredness and hopelessness.

Let us all mamas make a promise that we will not think of giving up on anything. We will keep trying and making it comfortable for our babies. We will try new things. I need you to at least try to follow this book and believe me you will feel a difference. Don't take it as a whole but break it into smaller portions and try everything. If an inexperienced mama like me can do it without any guidance and become a pro, what will hinder you after being taught everything with this book!

REFERENCES

(n.d.). Retrieved from https://themilkmeg.com: https://themilkmeg.com/will-introducing-bottle-ruin-chances-breastfeeding/

(2017, Sep 20). Retrieved from https://thenaturalparentmagazine.com: https://thenaturalparentmagazine.com/breastfeeding-aversion-agitation-baa/2/

(2018, Dec 11). Retrieved from https://www.healthline.com: https://www.healthline.com/health/childrens-health/home-made-baby-food-recipes#takeaway

(2018, August 24). Retrieved from https://www.healthychildren.org: https://www.healthychildren.org/English/ages-stages/baby/formula-feeding/Pages/Amount-and-Schedule-of-Formula-Feedings.aspx

(2019, Feb 11). Retrieved from https://www.who.int: https://www.who.int/elena/titles/breastfeeding_inability/en/

(2019, Oct 17). Retrieved from https://www.nhs.uk: https://www.nhs.uk/conditions/baby/breastfeeding-and-bottle-feeding/bottle-feeding/types-of-formula/

(2019, May 09). Retrieved from https://www.tommys.org: https://www.tommys.org/pregnancy-information/after-birth/feeding-your-baby/formula-feeding

(2019, August 27). Retrieved from https://www.eatingwell.com: https://www.eatingwell.com/gallery/13738/american-classic-recipes-that-kids-love/

(2020, Nov 3). Retrieved from https://www.pumpstation.com: https://www.pumpstation.com/blogs/articles/offering-a-breastfed-baby-a-bottle

(2020). Retrieved from https://babyfoode.com: https://baby-foode.com/blog/ultimate-guide-on-how-to-make-and-serve-homemade-baby-food-without-stressing-out-about-it/

(2020, May 18). Retrieved from https://raisingchildren.net.au: https://raisingchildren.net.au/babies/breastfeeding-bottle-feeding-solids/solids-drinks/introducing-solids

(2020). Retrieved from https://www.meandmychild.co.nz: https://www.meandmychild.co.nz/infant/feeding-your-baby/choosing-right-formula

(2021, July 1). Retrieved from https://raisingchildren.net.au: https://raisingchildren.net.au/newborns/breastfeeding-bottle-feeding/bottle-feeding/giving-the-bottle

(2021). Retrieved from https://www.medela.com: https://www.medela.com/breastfeeding-professionals/prod-ucts/feeding/supplemental-nursing-system

(2021). Retrieved from https://milkbarbreastpumps.com.au: https://milkbarbreastpumps.com.au/blogs/news/using-a-supplemental-nursing-system-or-sns

(2021, March 17). Retrieved from https://www.healthychildren.org: https://www.healthychildren.org/English/ages-stages/baby/feeding-nutrition/Pages/Starting-Solid-Foods.aspx

(2021, August 24). Retrieved from https://www.cdc.gov: https://www.cdc.gov/nutrition/infantandtoddlernutrition/foods-and-drinks/when-to-introduce-solid-foods.html

(2021, May 20). Retrieved from https://www.mayoclinic.org: https://www.mayoclinic.org/healthy-lifestyle/infant-and-toddler-health/in-depth/healthy-baby/art-20046200

(2021). Retrieved from https://thedgafmom.com: https://thedgafmom.com/theblog/choosing-the-right-formula-for-your-baby

A, M. (2020, Feb 07). *breastfeeding strike*. Retrieved from www.mayoclinic.org: https://www.mayoclinic.org/healthy-lifestyle/infant-and-toddler-health/expert-answers/breastfeeding-strike/faq-20058157

Angela. (n.d.). Retrieved from https://www.happyfamilyorganics.com: https://www.happyfamilyorganics.com/learning-center/recipes-meal-plans/meal-plan/12-months-meal-plan/

Anzilotti, A. W. (2020, Jan). *Postpartum depression*. Retrieved from www.kidshealth.org: https://kidshealth.org/en/parents/ppd.html

Association. (2019, May). *Baby won't breastfeed*. Retrieved from www.breastfeeding.asn.au: https://www.breastfeeding.asn.au/bf-info/breast-refusal

Baby, F. (2020, Feb 25). Retrieved from https://kellymom.com: https://kellymom.com/bf/pumpingmoms/feeding-tools/bottle-feeding/

Ben-Joseph, E. P. (2020). Retrieved from https://kidshealth.org: https://kidshealth.org/en/parents/breast-bottle-feeding.html

Bilich, K. A. (2005, Oct 3). Retrieved from https://www.parents.com: https://www.parents.com/baby/feeding/bottlefeeding/your-step-by-step-guide-to-bottlefeeding/

Bonyata, K. (2019, Jan 15). *Breastfeeding*. Retrieved from www.kellymom.com: https://kellymom.com/ages/older-infant/babyselfwean/

Bottle Feeding. (2020). Retrieved from https://www.betterhealth.vic.gov.au: https://www.betterhealth.vic.gov.au/health/healthyliving/bottle-feeding-nutrition-and-safety

bottle, F. f. (2021, July 12). Retrieved from https://www.cdc.gov: https://www.cdc.gov/nutrition/infantandtoddlernutrition/bottle-feeding/index.html

Brannan, D. (2015, Sep). Retrieved from https://www.webmd.com: https://www.webmd.com/parenting/baby/features/making-baby-food#3

Bruce, D. F. (2020, Aug 4). *postpartum depression*. Retrieved from www.webmd.com: https://www.webmd.com/depression/guide/postpartum-depression

Buchanan, J. (n.d.). Retrieved from https://www.chla.org: https://www.chla.org/blog/rn-remedies/eight-tips-how-introduce-bottle-feeding

Bushell, S. (2020, May 25). Retrieved from https://www.childrensnutrition.co.uk: https://www.childrensnutrition.co.uk/full-blog/paced-feeding

centre, B. (2020). Retrieved from https://www.babycentre.co.uk: https://www.babycentre.co.uk/a8491/what-is-nipple-confusion

Champion, L. (2020, march 23). Retrieved from https://www.purewow.com: https://www.purewow.com/food/toddler-dinner-ideas

Clarke, E. (2018). Retrieved from https://www.wellplated.com/cinnamon-roasted-butternut-squash/: https://www.wellplated.com/cinnamon-roasted-butternut-squash/

Crider, C. (2020, March 29). *No milk.* Retrieved from https://www.healthline.com: https://www.healthline.com/health/breastfeeding/no-breast-milk-after-delivery-what-to-do

Fedding. (2020). Retrieved from https://www.askdrsears.com: https://www.askdrsears.com/topics/feeding-eating/breastfeeding/common-problems/nipple-confusion/

Felman, A. (2020, Sep 29). *What to know about PDD.* Retrieved from www.medicalnewstoday.com: https://www.medicalnewstoday.com/articles/237109

Gorin, A. (2021, March 29). Retrieved from https://www.parents.com: https://www.parents.com/baby/feeding/solid-foods/starting-solids-guide/

Health, T. P. (2003, Oct). *Postpartum Depression .* Retrieved from www.who.int: https://www.who.int/mental_health/prevention/suicide/lit_review_postpartum_depression.pdf

Hosseini, S. (2017, May 19). Retrieved from https://www.romper.com: https://www.romper.com/p/9-reasons-women-cant-breastfeed-why-you-shouldnt-shame-them-for-it-58095

Howland, G. (2020, August 3). Retrieved from https://www.mamanatural.com: https://www.mamanatural.com/paced-bottle-feeding/

Johnson, J. (2018, Nov 12). Retrieved from https://www.medicalnewstoday.com: https://www.medicalnewstoday.com/articles/320436

Karmel, A. (2020). Retrieved from https://www.annabelkarmel.com: https://www.annabelkarmel.com/recipes/chicken-apple-balls/

Kim, S. (2018, Dec 18). Retrieved from https://www.healthline.com: https://www.healthline.com/health/parenting/nipple-confusion#takeaway

Kirbie. (2019). Retrieved from https://kirbiecravings.com: https://kirbiecravings.com/zucchini-noodles-mac-cheese/

Kummar, M. (2016, April 21). Retrieved from https://michaelkummer.com: https://michaelkummer.com/health/nipple-confusion/

Lane, A. (2021, Jan 18). Retrieved from https://www.thebump.com: https://www.thebump.com/a/best-baby-spoons-bowls-plates

Levine, H. (2020, August 17). Retrieved from https://www.whattoexpect.com: https://www.whattoexpect.com/first-year/breastfeeding/problems/

Lilli. (2021). Retrieved from https://www.llli.org: https://www.llli.org/breastfeeding-info/nipple-confusion/

McDowell, E. (n.d.). Retrieved from https://www.purewow.com: https://www.purewow.com/recipes/One-Pot-Mac-and-Cheese

Medela. (2021). Retrieved from https://www.medela.us: https://www.medela.us/breastfeeding/articles/what-is-nipple-confusion-and-how-to-resolve-it

Mitri, M. (n.d.). Retrieved from https://elsenutrition.com: https://elsenutrition.com/blogs/news/why-choose-an-organic-baby-formula

Murray, D. (2020, Dec 10). *Breastfeeding.* Retrieved from www.verywellfamily.com: https://www.verywellfamily.com/breast-refusal-431907

Murray, D. (2021, April 10). *Can't Breastfeed.* Retrieved from https://www.verywellfamily.com: https://www.verywellfamily.com/why-some-women-cant-breastfeed-4153606

Mylnek, A. (2017, April 26). Retrieved from https://www.todaysparent.com: https://www.todaysparent.com/baby/breastfeeding/supplemental-nursing-system-sns/

Nall, R. (2015, 25 Sep). Retrieved from https://www.healthline.com: https://www.healthline.com/health/parenting/paced-bottle-feeding#The-Takeaway

O'Connor, A. (2020, August 10). Retrieved from https://www.whattoexpect.com: https://www.whattoexpect.com/first-year/breastfeeding/breastfeeding-guide/why-you-might-not-be-able-to-breastfeed.aspx

Palangian, A. (2020, Jan 22). Retrieved from https://www.yummytoddlerfood.com: https://www.yummytoddlerfood.com/homemade-baby-food/

Patel, O. (2017, Nov 8). *Disliking Btreastmilk.* Retrieved from www.romper.com: https://www.romper.com/p/do-babies-ever-dislike-the-taste-of-your-breast-milk-expert-explains-3241471

Pearson-Glaze, P. (2020, June 17). Retrieved from https://breastfeeding.support: https://breastfeeding.support/supplementing-at-the-breast/

Pearson-Glaze, P. (2020, June 17). Retrieved from https://breastfeeding.support: https://breastfeeding.support/homemade-supplemental-nursing-system/

Petre, A. (2020, Feb 25). Retrieved from https://www.healthline.com: https://www.healthline.com/nutrition/soy-formula#when-to-avoid-it

Pietangelo, A. (2016, Dec 6). *Everything about postpartum depression.* Retrieved from www.healthline.com: https://www.healthline.com/health/depression/postpartum-depression#tips

Postapartum depression . (2021, July). Retrieved from www.helpguide.org: https://www.helpguide.org/articles/depression/postpartum-depression-and-the-baby-blues.htm

Postpartum Depression . (2019, March). Retrieved from www.marchofdimes.org: https://www.marchofdimes.org/pregnancy/postpartum-depression.aspx#

Postpartum depression . (2020, May 14). Retrieved from www.cdc.gov: https://www.cdc.gov/reproductivehealth/depression/index.htm

Postpartum Depression. (2019, May 14). Retrieved from www.womenshealth.gov: https://www.womenshealth.gov/mental-health/mental-health-conditions/postpartum-depression

Resnick, M. (2021, Feb 23). Retrieved from https://www.whattoexpect.com: https://www.whattoexpect.com/first-year/feeding-your-baby/milk-allergy-in-infants.aspx

Roth, M. (2021, Feb 3). *Baby crying while breastfeeding.* Retrieved from www.momlovesbest.com: https://momlovesbest.com/fussy-baby-while-breastfeeding

Ruiz, E. (2019, Feb 11). *Breastfeeding not working*. Retrieved from www.babygaga.com: https://www.babygaga.com/20-signs-the-breastmilk-is-not-working-for-the-baby/

Sears, D. (n.d.). Retrieved from https://www.askdrsears.com: https://www.askdrsears.com/topics/feeding-eating/breastfeeding/faqs/alternatives-bottles/

Staff. (n.d.). Retrieved from https://www.mayoclinic.org: https://www.mayoclinic.org/healthy-lifestyle/infant-and-toddler-health/in-depth/infant-formula/art-20045791

staff, H. (2020, Oct 8). Retrieved from https://www.uofmhealth.org: https://www.uofmhealth.org/health-library/hw133953

Stobbe, H. (2021). Retrieved from https://themamacoach.com: https://themamacoach.com/supplemental-nursing-system-what-is-it-and-when-is-it-used/

taylor, M. (2021, May 6). Retrieved from https://www.whattoexpect.com: https://www.whattoexpect.com/first-year/bottle-feeding/introducing-the-bottle-to-baby/

Taylor, M. (2021, July 20). Retrieved from https://www.whattoexpect.com: https://www.whattoexpect.com/first-year/how-much-formula-does-your-baby-need

Tonya. (2019, May 10). Retrieved from https://www.writermomforhire.com: https://www.writermomforhire.com/nursing-aversion/

Torres, F. (2020, Oct). *Depression* . Retrieved from www.psychiatry.org: https://www.psychiatry.org/patients-families/postpartum-depression/what-is-postpartum-depression

Weisenberger, J. (2019, Dec 17). Retrieved from https://www.eatright.org: https://www.eatright.org/food/planning-and-prep/snack-and-meal-ideas/how-to-make-home-made-baby-food

Wilson, K. (n.d.). Retrieved from https://newbornbaby.com.au: https://newbornbaby.com.au/newborn-overview/baby-formula/how-to-choose-the-right-baby-formula/

Wisner, W. (2019, August 27). Retrieved from https://www.verywellfamily.com: https://www.verywellfamily.com/paced-bottle-feeding-4691068

Yate, Z. (n.d.). Retrieved from https://kellymom.com: https://kellymom.com/bf/concerns/mother/breastfeeding-nursing-aversion-agitation-baa/

Yate, Z. (2020, Sep 7). Retrieved from https://www.positive-birthmovement.org: https://www.positivebirthmovement.org/ten-things-you-dont-expect-about-breastfeeding-aversion/

The clinic, C. (2018, January 01). *Benefits of breastfeeding.* Retrieved from clevelandclinic.org: https://my.clevelandclinic.org/health/articles/15274-the-benefits-of-breastfeeding-for-baby-- for-mom

Danny. (2021, Sep 14). *Inverted nipples.* Retrieved from webmd.com:

https://www.webmd.com/women/inverted-nipples-causes

Jacobson, J. D. (2020, May 10). *Breastfeeding-selfcare.* Retrieved from www.medlineolus.gov: https://medlineplus.gov/ency/patientinstructions/000631.htm

LisaG. (2019, june 2). *Preparing to Breastfeed Baby.* Retrieved from birth eat love : https://www.birtheatlove.com/preparing-to-breastfeed-baby/

LISAG. (2019, june 2). *preparing to breastfeed baby.* Retrieved from birtheastlove.com: https://www.birtheatlove.com/pre-paring-to-breastfeed-baby/

list, T. m. (2020, August 31). *breastfeeding essentials*. Retrieved from themamaslist.com: https://www.themammaslist.com/top-12-breastfeeding-products-first-year/

mommy, C. t. (2019, november 2). *19 breastfeeding tips*. Retrieved from mommy on purpose: https://mommyonpurpose.com/19-awesome-breastfeeding-tips-hacks-new

moms/?epik=dj0yJnU9US1DcFFoZ29yYzNIOGJfUkgwXzc0-Zl91b29pSzdEc2QmcD0wJm49azVRNGl RTzA2R0ZCMlpSc-XVzeHFDQSZ0PUFBQUFBR0VRNnM4

Nall, R. (2020, Feb). *Cracked nipples, treatment*. Retrieved from medicalnewstoday.com: https://www.medicalnewstoday.-com/articles/cracked-nipples#summary

Salon, L. (2013, Feb 23). Breastfeeding: An overview of oral and general health benefits. *The Journal of the American Dental Association*, **143-151. Retrieved from ScienceDirect.com: https://www.sciencedirect.com/ science/article/abs/pii/S0002817714606152**

Sutter. (n.d.). *breastmilk production*. Retrieved from sutter-health.org:

https://www.sutterhealth.org/health/newborns/breast-milk-production

WebMD. (2021, january 10). *Breastfeeding* . Retrieved from webmd.com:

https://www.webmd.com/parenting/baby/nursing-basics#1

ABOUT THE AUTHOR

I am KIMBERLY NICOLE WHITTAKER, mother of three; two gorgeous girls and one handsome boy. Being a mother of three has made me realize that we mothers have to go through a lot for feeding our babies. Especially the first 2 years of a baby's life are most delicate and sensitive to handle. But I am glad that I am writing this book for all the mamas out there so that I would share my experiences of feeding a baby from day one to two years old. I have gone through many struggles in handling the baby for breastfeeding and selecting a formula, solid foods, and recipes for my babies and I don't want any mother to go through the same struggle. I found myself illiterate at many steps that I don't know anything about feeding my baby. That was the moment when I decided to write this book for all the mothers so that they won't feel left out or empty-handed while dealing with procedures of feeding a baby. I am hoping that you will feel lucky after reading this book and might become a super mom.

Made in the USA
Middletown, DE
06 September 2022